Brian and Eileen Anderson

walk & eat
RHODES

2 CONTENTS

This pocket guide is designed to add another dimension to a walking holiday on Rhodes. It caters for those who just want to stroll, those who may prefer a longer walk — or even those who are just looking for recommendations on where to eat!

Whether you fly out for a week or a fortnight, you have in your hand enough walks, excursions, tavernas or restaurants and recipes to last throughout — so you can choose the most appealing.

The highlights at a glance:
- 12 varied day walks, each with topographical map or plan
- 2 excursions — one on Rhodes and one exploring a different Greek island
- recommended cafés, tavernas, restaurants and hotels
- recipes to make at your self-catering base or back home
- advice for those on special diets and for wheat-, gluten- and dairy-free eating and shopping on the island

INTRO

THE WALKS

Rhodes is a surprisingly large island, with tourism generally settled around the coastal regions. Apart from exploring the old medieval town of Rhodes, the walks in this book have been chosen mainly to visit well-known beauty spots or the island's spectacular countryside regions — places most tourists never see.

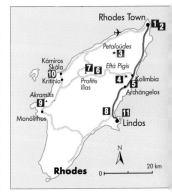

Most walks can be reached by bus; for the others (all circular) you will need to use a hire car or taxi.

The walks are of varying distance and range from easy to moderate. The interior of the island is hilly to mountainous, so the *character* of the walks varies considerably. The walk *gradings* in this book all assume comfortable walking conditions, so please remember that while the uphill sections mostly cause no problems for fairly active people when temperatures are comfortable, they can be much more stressful when temperatures rise towards summer heat.

THE EXCURSIONS

Two 'days out' are described. The first is the spectacular and beautiful village of Líndos, where there is an ancient acropolis to explore, colourful and crowded narrow shopping streets to browse, and a beach waiting for you when relaxing becomes a priority. There is a huge selection of places to eat here; we have highlighted one or two. If you prefer a walk before lunch, Walk 11 starts and finishes in Líndos, while Walk 8 ends here.

The second excursion is to the little-known and most easterly of all Greece's islands, Kastellórizo. It's reached by fast catamaran, leaving a good five hours for exploration. The atmospheric harbour itself might be enough to captivate most visitors, but we feature a short walk with a castle, viewpoints, churches and a grain mill. And, of course, a restaurant where you can enjoy good, genuine Greek food.

THE RESTAURANTS AND TAVERNAS

There are hundreds if not

Other excursions

A number of other Greek islands can be visited from Rhodes. **Sími** is relatively close, and the trip there is a long-standing favourite. The main harbour town stacks up the hillside, one house on top of another, in a most breathtaking fashion. It's a highly recommended trip for those who haven't had the opportunity to visit before.

The introduction of faster catamarans has brought more islands within the reach of day trips, for instance **Nísyros, Tínos, Kos, Kálymnos, Léros**; you could even go to **Marmaris in Turkey**.

Hálki is also nearby, suitable for a day trip, with several ferries from Kámiros Skála daily in high season (the crossing takes 45min-1h). It's also possible from Rhodes Town, but crossings are less frequent and take about 1h15min. Check details at the Tourist Office.

thousands of restaurants and tavernas on Rhodes. Many simply serve the needs of a passing trade without ever striving for customer loyalty. Some restaurants turn away from their cultural roots to offer an 'international cuisine'. This generally means that you can enjoy familiar dishes you might find at home, like peppered steaks or chicken Kiev. Many visitors enjoy this type of food, but there is no place for it in

Taverna sign, Líndos

this book. All, or at least many of the restaurants *(estiatório)* and tavernas we have discounted probably serve excellent food in their style, but we were searching for something quite special — restaurants and tavernas offering a good standard of traditional Greek cuisine, preferably with a focus on Rhodian influences. The use of fresh ingredients was another guiding principle, and this is something to which the Greeks themselves pay a good deal of attention when they eat out. It's usually a good sign when you see a taverna full of locals!

A taverna is a down-to-earth restaurant. In a restaurant you would expect to find your table set with cutlery and glasses and the staff to be more attentive than may be the case in a taverna. The restaurant menu, too, might be more extensive and include a selection of international dishes. A taverna offers a more relaxed, laid-back atmosphere.

Normally, you sit at an empty table initially; it might have a tablecloth covered with a plastic sheet, but nothing else. A waiter then appears with a fresh paper cloth and, after your order is placed, a bread basket arrives with knives and forks included within. Wine glasses in tavernas are traditionally small tumblers, but more are converting to small wine glasses.

Restaurants are mostly associated with larger towns on the island, whereas tavernas can be found everywhere, and they are *all* you will find in the smaller villages and country areas. *And note,* by the way: while a fish taverna *(psarotavérna)* specialises in fish, it will often have grilled meat on offer.

For each of the featured restaurants and tavernas we generally say why we like them and, in a few cases,

Price guide

Restaurants and tavernas aren't graded or classified by the tourist authorities as they once were, and are no longer subject to price controls. In spite of this, the prices between the various establishments remain surprisingly similar. In general terms, it's much cheaper eating on Rhodes than at home.

The price guides in this book (€ to €€€) indicate 'very reasonable' to 'fairly pricey'. Remember that this guide relates not to prices at home, but to *prices on Rhodes*. The majority of establishments fall into the 'average' category, indicated by €€. Even so, it's always possible to enjoy a relatively inexpensive meal in a top restaurant by choosing carefully from the menu. There's usually a large choice of inexpensive starter dishes which can easily make up a satisfying meal.

include a mini-menu listing specialities and/or exceptional dishes. But unlike other books in this series, we haven't included a great many taverna menus, because they are very similar all round the island.

Please be aware that no restaurant or taverna has paid in cash or in kind to be included in this guide.

THE RECIPES

Most of the recipes for Greek dishes are fairly well known, but many chefs tweak recipes, often with the use of herbs and spices, to give their dish a special flavour. Only a few of the restaurants we visited seemed willing to share their recipes, possibly because they are not written down but simply passed down through the family. There was also a language barrier when it came to fine details. Many of these restaurants and tavernas are entirely staffed by family. Even Greek cookery books have different recipes for the same dish.

We have guessed at the 'secret' ingredients and made all the recipes at home to our own satisfaction. Remember, when you're dining by the edge of the sea, listening to the soft music of lapping waves and watching the sun suffusing the sky with hues of orange and purple as it sinks below a wine-dark sea … the food may taste better than it really is!

Unfortunately, self-catering on a hot Greek island like Rhodes usually means basic equipment — enough to put a breakfast together, but not enough try out our hot recipes. There are usually only two hot plates — one small, for making Greek coffee, and one large. Not to mention the lack of suitable utensils. You'd have to find yourself in really up-market self-catering accommodation to encounter a full cooker!

One-pan meals, fried squid and fried courgettes *can* easily be made on one plate, however. (By the way, olive oil isn't good for frying at high temperatures; it degrades too quickly. Greeks commonly use a lighter sunflower oil or similar for frying.) Cold dishes, on the other hand, *are* easy to prepare in self-catering. (You can buy ready-cooked chickens in many of the larger supermarkets, too.) After a lunch out, a few cold dishes in the evening are ideal to finish off the day. At least when you're back home, trying out recipes you can't cope with in Greece, we might just be able to help you recapture that moment when the sun sank below the sea!

One quick and easy hot one-pan meal we *do* make in self-catering (and often at home) uses a rice-like pasta, *manéstra*. On Rhodes, this is also known by its Italian name, *orzo*. Look for it in the pasta section on supermarket shelves. It looks just like rice and comes in three sizes, small *(mikró)*, medium *(métrio)* and large *(megálo)*. Greek friends recommend the medium size for general use. Look for *kritharáki métrio* or the Italian *orzo medio,* both names under the *manéstra* umbrella. If you make this at home, however, you'll have to bring packets of pasta home from Greece unless you live near a Greek produce supplier or specialist delicatessen. Below is our basic 'throw together' recipe; experiment with it and come up with your own variations. We prefer *manéstra* to rice, as it absorbs flavours beautifully and is so easy to use. But, naturally, if you need a gluten-free option, it's a good recipe for a *risotto*.

Using 50-75 g of pasta per person, select some pre-cooked diced meats (chicken, turkey, pork, etc) and vegetables suitable for a stir fry (chopped onion, garlic, peppers, courgettes, celery, broccoli florets, frozen peas, whatever). Heat olive oil or sunflower oil in a large frying pan/wok, and gently stir fry the *fresh vegetables* with the pasta briefly. Then dissolve a stock cube or two in 250 ml water and stir into the pan. Add more water if necessary. Cover and simmer for 6 min. Stir and check the water, then add seasoning, herbs, the meat and the frozen peas (if used). Cover, bring back to a simmer, and cook a further 5 min. The pasta should be soft if the dish is ready and the moisture absorbed. Serve on its own or with crusty bread and green salad.

Manéstra

EATING GREEK

Eating out for Greek families is a social occasion. It's a pleasure just to watch them. Family and friends gather around the table, men and women sometimes choosing to segregate themselves, with the children up and down as children are. When the food arrives, it's placed in the centre of the table for all to share. Plate after plate arrives until there's hardly room left. The chatter is long and loud, and the pace of eating is slow. Hot food cooling is of no concern. If it's a festive occasion, impromptu Greek dancing quite often follows.

Visitors, on the other hand, usually order a Greek salad for one person, perhaps a *tzatzíki* for another and so on. But there are so many different dishes and flavours to enjoy, it makes sense to **put all the starters in the middle and share**. If you indicate that you would like to eat this way, the waiter will bring small empty plates for each person. Even with only two of you dining, two or three starters can be tried — but it's even better with four or more people eating. After the starters, it's much more acceptable to order individual main courses, although these can be treated in the same way as *mezédes* (appetizers) and shared. We became so used to sharing when living in Greece that we now often share starters and sweets — even in restaurants at home.

After decades of tourism, many tavernas now appreciate that you may not want every course you order to arrive at the same time. But some, especially in country areas, may *not* understand this, so it is best to order *mezédes* first, then order the rest later — or say *argótera* (later) for main courses, etc.

The Greeks **order certain dishes by weight**, usually lamb, pork chops or *kalamári* — all of which will be ordered by the kilo. A half kilo is usually plenty for two people and can be cheaper than ordering by the portion. Fish almost always appears on the menu priced by the kilo. It sometimes looks very expensive when you see the kilo price, but the fish will be weighed and a portion size is usually 300-400 g. If the fish you have chosen is particularly large, the waiter will weigh it for you and tell you its cost to get your agreement.

On the whole, most tavernas are honest about whether or not their **squid (*kalamári*)** is fresh *(fresko)* or frozen *(katepsigmeno)*. Unfortunately, especially in tourist areas, unscrupulous owners may charge for fresh, at the more expensive price, when you've been given frozen. (We were once almost caught this way but, since we were sure of our ground, we insisted on only paying the price for frozen squid. If you feel unhappy, ask for

the complaints book which
they must produce by law.)
Fresh squid usually comes as
one piece, lightly fried and
melt-in-the-mouth tender. It
can be served in rings, but if it
is, they will not be heavily
breaded or too uniform. You
can ask to see the piece being cooked
for you. Frozen squid is often rub-
bery and comes in fairly uniform,
crumbed rings. (We did have excellent frozen squid at the Oasis
Taverna in Old Rhodes Town,
however, and the proprietor told us
it had to be specially cut and frozen
properly to be tender.)

Fresh *kalamári* — at the
market and cooked (note the
large piece). Frozen *kalamári*
is shown on page 83.

RHODIAN FOOD

Rhodian food mirrors traditional Greek cuisine, but not
necessarily the full spectrum of dishes, and there are a couple of
Rhodian specialities not widely found elsewhere. One is
pitaroúdia (chickpea cakes), similar to potato cakes, but flatter. In
fact, chickpeas appear in many island recipes. This is good news
for those on gluten-free diets, but always ask if any wheat flour
has been added.

Over the many years we've been travelling to Greece and
enjoying Greek food, the cuisine has always remained tradi-

tional and constant. But the influence of British high-profile TV cookery programmes has spread far and wide. Similar programmes on Greek television have brought a more progressive influence into the country's cuisine, and traditional dishes have started to evolve. This is very noticeable in the salads, for instance, which have improved in variety and content.

Herbs and spices are intrinsic elements in Greek cooking, especially oregano, thyme and dill, which are sprinkled on everything grilled. On Rhodes, mint (spearmint) is more favoured, especially for sprinkling on cheese and salads. Cumin and *bakári* (allspice) are the two most frequently used spices.

THE MENU

Life would be simpler if the menu (*katálogos*) in Greece was always set out in the familiar way of starters, main courses and sweets. It sometimes is, but then often further divided or subdivided. Fortunately, menus are usually available in English — although they are not always as helpful as they might be. A number of dishes have no direct equivalent. *Hórta (xórta),* for

Hórta

example, is a dish variously described as boiled greens or spinach. It's the green leaves of the dandelion family (but not strictly dandelions), sometimes collected wild, which are boiled, strained, seasoned, amply tossed in olive oil and lemon juice and served as a single vegetable dish. Very good if it's fresh — a great favourite with the Greeks, and one of our favourites too. Similarly, familiar dishes such as *mousaká* are described in all sorts of ways — 'meat pie with béchamel sauce' is fairly typical.

The **starters** (*orektiká*) make up the most interesting section, and the list should be quite long. Salads are usually listed here, but may appear in their own section; the same is true for cheese dishes. Starters are a boon for vegetarians and vegans and often suitable for those on gluten-free diets, since many are vegetables served as single dishes — for instance giant butter beans (*gígantes*), beetroot cooked with their leaves *(patzária)*, fried courgettes *(kolokithákia tiganitá)*, fried aubergines (*melitzana tiganitá*) and the already-mentioned *hórta*. There's an interesting array of dips too, from the familiar *taramasaláta* (cod's roe) and *tzatzíki* (yoghourt/cucumber/garlic) to aubergine dip (*melitza-nosaláta*) and garlic/mashed potato (*skordaliá*). On Rhodes *skordaliá* is often served to complement other dishes, like beetroot and, traditionally, cod fish. These dips sometimes appear under the salad list. Still more starter treats include chick pea *keftédes (revithokeftédes)*, which are one of our favourites and easy to make. There is a similar speciality only found on Rhodes, *pitaroúdia* (see recipe on page 66). Everybody has their own recipe and it may or may not contain chick peas.

Cheese (*tirí*) dishes on the starters list include *féta* sprinkled with herbs and drizzled with olive oil, *saganáki* (fried *féta* — or another cheese), *saganáki sto foúrno* (oven-baked *féta* with tomatoes and peppers, often spicy), grilled *haloúmi* (a dish borrowed from Cyprus, which is popular on Rhodes), *tirosaláta* (a spicy cheese dip), and *tirokeftédes* (cheese croquettes).

Greek **salad** (*horiátiki saláta*) is synonymous with Greek cuisine for most visitors. There is no standard; it depends on the season, but tomato, cucumber and olives are ever-present, topped by a lump of *féta* cheese and often liberally soaked in olive oil and vinegar. Sometimes it can be a meal in itself. It's on every menu and serves as a useful price comparison between tavernas. Very often we prefer just to have a salad of tomato and cucumber *(domáta/angoúri)*. One salad mostly ignored by visitors, but popular with the Greeks, is lettuce salad *(maroúli saláta)*. It doesn't sound very exciting, but is really tasty the way it's prepared (see page 90). Salads are slowly evolving, cherry tomatoes replacing or supplementing the large Mediterranean tomato, rocket leaves and roasted aubergine adding much more variety.

The **main courses** are listed under *entrádes*, grills and/or meat *(kréas)*, or there may be just one list. Normally, under the *entrádes* you can expect to find **Greek specialities** like *mousakás*, *stifádo* (a veal and shallot stew), *kokkinistó* (veal stew with tomatoes) and *giouvétsi* (veal in a clay pot with *manéstra*, the rice-like pasta mentioned on page 10); the **grills** are found in other sections. **Fish** *(psári)* or **seafood** *(thalasiná)* are normally listed separately.

Beef is served in the form of veal *(moskári)* — beef from a milk-weaned yearling animal. Steaks seem to appear on restaurant menus, whereas tavernas stick with chops *(brizóla)* which are large and meaty. Pork chops *(hoiriní brizóla)* and lamb cutlets *(païdákia)* are popular, but these meats are also served on skewers as *souvláki*. Chicken and fish are also sometimes served this way. Goat *(katsíki)* is popular on Rhodes, and is eaten as chops or a roast which, like lamb, can be ordered by the kilo or by the portion *(merída)*.

Poultry is almost invariably chicken *(kotópoulo)*, but turkey *(galópoula)* is found occasionally.

On a visit to a good supermarket or a market, you will see fresh vegetables in abundance, but you are unlikely to see many **vegetables** with your main course — if any. Chips are fairly ubiquitous, but some dishes like squid *(kalamári)* are served without, so you may need to enquire. Chips *(patátes tiganités)* are always available as a side order with your starters or main course. If you just ask for *patátes,* it's generally understood you want *chips.*

On Rhodes it's fairly typical to find **fish restaurants around coastal regions**. Although predominantly serving fish, fish restaurants invariably offer a selection of meat dishes. There is also a distinct **'meat belt'** on Rhodes, which runs down along the **mountain areas**, at places like Émbonas and Apóllona. Here local lamb and goat are specialities — as well as very hearty village sausage.

Desserts are listed under *glyká,* which means 'sweet'. The Greeks have a sweet tooth and love their sweets soaked in syrup and honey. But these sweets are not a major feature of taverna menus and sometimes don't appear at all. Very often the taverna owner will bring complementary fresh fruit, depending on the season. It might be grapes, watermelon or oranges, but one of our favourites is sliced apple dusted with cinnamon and drizzled with honey. Restaurants usually offer a better menu for desserts.

Greek honey sweets

One of the most popular sweets with tourists is yoghurt and honey which may be topped with walnuts (see page 97). It's not really a traditional Greek sweet, but a response to its immense popularity with visitors. Even if not on the menu it can often be rustled up for you, since the taverna is likely to have a stock of thick, strained yoghurt for making *tzatzíki*.

Baklavá, *kataïfi* and *halvá* are amongst the intensely sweet sweets. *Baklavá*, multi-layered filo pastry sandwiching finely chopped almonds or walnuts, rich in butter and soaked in sugar/honey syrup, finds many devotees (125 g = 695 calories). *Kataïfi*, best described as small shredded wheats (actually a pastry), soaked in sugar/honey syrup appeals to the same group of supporters, as does the *halvá*, a brown, sugar-rich sesame seed confection which is poured into a mould to set.

Galaktoboúriko (recipe on page 85) comes in much lower down the calorie scale. It's vanilla custard sandwiched between layers of filo pastry. *Loukoumádes*, batter balls soaked in honey syrup, is another of the dessert offerings.

Coffee *(kafé)* deserves a special mention. At one time, only 'Nes' (short for Nescafé or any instant coffee) was available: strong enough to 'stand up' the proverbial spoon, it was served with a glass of water. Nowadays, water is still often served, but other options such as filter and cappuccino are commonplace. *A word of caution:* Greek Nes (Nescafé) is stronger and more bitter than its UK equivalent, so use it sparingly when you buy it for use at your hotel or in self-catering.

If you do happen to be in an establishment which only serves Nes, and you're not a lover of very strong coffee, ask for it *elafrí*, weak. Another pitfall to watch out for is added sugar. The Greeks normally have sugar in their coffee, which is sometimes added automatically when it's made. As well as *elafrí,* you need to add *horís zákari* (without sugar). You may require your coffee with/without milk *(me/horís gála).*

Ordering a **Greek coffee** is quite different. Sugar is added during the preparation, so you need to specify *glykó* (sweet), *métrio* (medium) or *skéto* (without sugar). Greek coffee is never served with milk.

Tea *(tsái)* is widely available — even herbal teas — in restaurants and some cafés. But in some older establishments and in country areas, where tea drinkers are more of a rarity, the need for boiling water to make a decent 'cuppa' hasn't quite filtered through. Don't be surprised if your tea arrives lukewarm. *Zestó vrásto neró* (boiling water) and bubbling gestures with your hands might help!

Frappé

In the heat of summer this is a popular drink for Greeks as well as tourists. Easy to make yourself, either in one of the cheap plastic *frappé* shakers (available in supermarkets) or in a jar with a screw cap. For each *frappé*, put a teaspoon of instant coffee in the container, add ice cubes then half water and half milk (fresh milk, or the Greek evaporated milk called *Noynoy*, or soya), plus sugar if wanted. Shake vigorously until the coffee has dissolved and it's nice and frothy.

RHODIAN WINES

Vines are grown extensively in the mountainous regions around Émbonas, where there are a number of successful wine producers. Traditional grape varieties like *Athíri* and *Mandilária* have been grown on the island for centuries. *Mandilária*, it's said, was used to make wine drunk by the Knights of St John. These varieties still provide the bulk of wines made, but more international varieties are now being grown, like Cabernet Sauvignon and Grenache.

Athíri makes a very quaffable dry white wine and is widely used. Ílios and Ródos 2400 on the CAIR label both feature this grape, as does Athíri on the Emery label. Red wine drinkers will not be displeased with Chevalier de Rhodes, based on the *Mandilária* grape, from CAIR, or the Rodon Cabernet Sauvignon from Emery.

In spite of the best efforts of the wine producers to promote the leading labels, the bulk wine released for sale as house wine is virtually the same standard. It's so good and so much cheaper that everybody drinks it, and we have yet to have a house wine on Rhodes that disappointed us. The whites are especially good.

House wine is bought by the kilo, which is effectively the same as a litre. It's a hangover from the days when you went along to the shop with your jug to buy wine from the barrel. With four people your first order would be a kilo, but two might start with a half-kilo *(misó kiló)* and take it from there. The wine often comes in a metal jug or, sometimes, a ceramic jug.

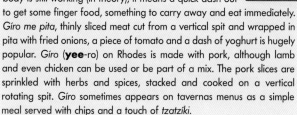

Fast food, Greek-style

The Greeks have been in the fast food market longer than anyone can remember. The pattern of their working life has always been (and still is for most) an early start and an early finish. An early start does not leave time for breakfast, and an early finish means there is time for a good lunch, usually between 2 and 3 in the afternoon.

A mid-morning snack replaces breakfast. Since everybody is still working (in theory), it means a quick dash out to get some finger food, something to carry away and eat immediately. *Gíro me pita*, thinly sliced meat cut from a vertical spit and wrapped in pita with fried onions, a piece of tomato and a dash of yoghurt is hugely popular. *Gíro* (**yee**-ro) on Rhodes is made with pork, although lamb and even chicken can be used or be part of a mix. The pork slices are sprinkled with herbs and spices, stacked and cooked on a vertical rotating spit. *Gíro* sometimes appears on tavernas menus as a simple meal served with chips and a touch of *tzatzíki*.

Pies are a great favourite too, especially *tirópita* (cheese), *spanakópita* (spinach, sometimes with cheese and egg) and *kréatopita* (minced meat). All are made with several layers of filo pastry with the appropriate filling. *Spanakópita* (recipe page 137) is our favourite. Mostly they are individual pies but occasionally they may be made in a large tray and cut into slices (especially true of *spanakópita*).

Pizza, in mini size or slices, has made an appearance in the last decades and become a favourite. More traditional is *souvláki*, lumps of meat on a wooden skewer served with a chunk of bread or in a pita parcel like the *gíro*.

If you have time to wait five minutes, you can order *tost* (a toasted ham and cheese on unbuttered bread). You can specify the filling if you just want one or the other — or even a slice of tomato added.

There are pies for the sweet tooth, too: *mílopita* (apple pie) and, another favourite, *bougátza* (vanilla custard pie).

RETSINA, OUZO & SOUMA

It's said that resinated wine, or retsína, originated in the days before wine bottles, when wine was stored in jars or skins sealed with pine resin. When bottles came on the scene, the wine without the resin flavour was not universally popular, so retsína was born. It's generally much preferred by the Greeks — but less so on Rhodes, possibly because the quality of the house wines is so good. Provided the wine is only lightly resinated, it can be quite palatable, and the resin stabilises the wine — which gives it consistency. CAIR makes a good, refreshing retsína, but our favourite is Malamátina. Kourtáki is the best-known brand internationally, but this is moderately resinated and not the easiest retsína for the uninitiated to fall in love with at first sip! Often a pale-coloured retsína signifies less resin, making a more palatable drink for first-timers.

Oúzo is a drink for bright sunshine and bonding, Greek-style. This aniseed-flavoured drink is taken with ice and water and, traditionally, a few nibbles. There are still one or two *oúzeri* around, where you can sit with an oúzo and expect some free *mezédes* (*mezés* for short) — a little plate with a piece of cheese perhaps, a chunk of bread, maybe a few cold chips, or anything to hand. But this tradition is now only usual in country villages away from mass tourism.

When we lived on Lesvos some years ago, the locals insisted that Lesvos made the best oúzo in Greece. We put this down to local pride, but since then we have travelled to many other Greek islands and, sure enough, everybody tells us the best oúzo is from Lesvos. Oúzo 12, Mini and Barbayanni are all leading brands.

Soúma (called *tsípouro* on the Greek mainland and *tsikoudiá* on Crete) is an under-the-counter drink elsewhere, but not on Rhodes. It's made from the distillation of grape alcohol, often from small reject grapes, with flavourings added before distillation. Farmers around Siána on Rhodes were granted a licence by the Italians which was never rescinded, so they can make it legally. It's a powerful, colourless spirit drink which tends to lift the top off the head. Can be a good medicine in the mornings if you're feeling slightly lethargic!

PLANNING YOUR VISIT
When to go
Tourism on Rhodes is seasonal. Charter flights normally start towards the end of April and finish towards the end of October. It's easy enough to reach the island out of season or anytime by taking an international flight to Athens and an internal flight to Rhodes — a journey which can usually be achieved in one day.

The best time for walkers is **spring and autumn**. April is the finest month, especially for flower-lovers, but May is good too. The heat starts to build in June and at some point it becomes too hot to enjoy strenuous walks, but some of the easy or short walks remain possible, especially with an early start. July, August and early September are generally too hot for walking unless you are prepared to rise with the sun and walk very, very early in the morning. Walking in the full heat of the sun in this period is risking serious heat exhaustion and is *most definitely*

not recommended. Temperatures decline slowly throughout September, and usually by the middle of the month walking is back on the agenda — but it may still be advisable to avoid strenuous walks for a time. By October the temperatures are usually back to the mid or low 20s, and walking becomes a pleasure again.

Eating is a pleasure to be enjoyed anytime of the year so, even if it's too hot to walk, you might still want to try some of our suggested restaurants and tavernas!

Where to stay

There are two clusters of tourist accommodation on the island. The main cluster is around the northern tip, around Rhodes Town, starting at Triánda/Ixiá on the west-facing side of the island and continuing through Rhodes Town down the eastern side through Kalithéa to Faliráki and Kolímbia. The other cluster is around Líndos.

Breezy **Ixiá** catches the prevailing westerlies which pleasantly moderates the heat of summer. It's a resort favoured by many of the island's most luxurious hotels, like the Amathus Elite Suites (see page 50), which we visit for its excellent Varkarola Taverna. It's well connected by bus to Rhodes Town. **Rhodes Town** has many hotels, which may be ideal if you like a busy town atmosphere. Since this is the hub of the island bus service, it's easy to get public transport to the various walks from here.

The main bus service runs down the eastern side of the island from Rhodes to Líndos, so many resorts on the east coast are well placed for bus connections. Moving down the eastern side of the island, **Kalithéa** is a relatively small resort, but the next one, Faliráki, is much bigger. In spite of bad press over recent years, **Faliráki** is still a great resort with perhaps the best beach on the island. For a peaceful existence, choose a hotel on the outskirts. There are some good hotels located on the coastal strip just north of Faliráki — just keep out of the centre at night. In any case, it's a very quiet resort in the walking season and only becomes rowdy in the height of summer when the party animals arrive in numbers. Now with a permanent police presence in the resort, the troublesome element has been mostly eliminated.

Still on the east coast, and south of Faliráki, lie **Afándou** and **Kolímbia**. These two resorts have been growing steadily in recent years, but are not large like Faliráki. Many, but not all buses running between Rhodes and Líndos call in at Kolímbia Beach, but it's reasonably well served in season. Afándou is more of a problem: buses run along the main road behind the resort, but at present don't turn off along the beach road, so it's at least a 10-15 minute walk to the beach.

The second cluster of resorts is well down the eastern side of the island — Líndos, Péfkos and Lárdos. **Líndos**, lying in a sweeping bay overlooked by an ancient acropolis, is a spectacular resort and a 'must' place to visit. It's one of the two excursions we have chosen. **Péfkos** and **Lárdos** lie a little further south. Although well connected by bus to Rhodes Town, these two resorts are a little remote from our walks, the only two neaby being Walks 8 and 11.

What to take

There is no special dress code for dining, except that shorts are not always appreciated in restaurants and some tavernas during the evening. It's useful for men to pack at least one tie, on a just-in-case basis, especially if a casino visit is on the cards.

It's more important to concentrate on packing suitable walking gear. Walking boots are the footwear we most strongly recommend, but not all the walks demand them. Some of the track walks are fairly easy underfoot, and for these we prefer **walking shoes** or specialist walking trainers, especially if the weather is hot. Each person should carry a **small rucksack** and it's advisable to pack it with a **sunhat**, **suncream**, **first-aid kit** and some extra **warm clothing**. A **long-sleeved shirt** and **long trousers** should be worn or carried for sun protection and for walking through spiny vegetation. You should always carry a **mobile** (the **emergency number** on Rhodes is 112) or a **smartphone** (to access the internet or use our GPS tracks).

Depending on the season, you may also need lightweight **rainwear** and a lightweight folding **umbrella**. Some of our walks end up at a beach, so **swimwear** could be usefully included. A reliable litre-size **water bottle** is well worth packing, although

Beach bar, Ixiá

small, easily carried bottles of water can be bought all over the island. *It is imperative that each walker carries at least a half-litre of water — a full litre or more when the weather is hot.*

Planning your walks

Look over the walks you plan to take in advance, to check out **transport**. Most of the walks can be reached by public transport, but the remainder will require a hire car or taxi.

We have **graded** the walks with the weekend walker in mind, *based on an ambient temperature below the mid 20s C*. When temperatures rise above this level, walkers expend more energy simply keeping cool, and uphill walking and steep downhills are much more tiring. The **walking times** given at certain points always refer to the total walking time from the start and are based on an average rate of 4km per hour and allowing an extra 15min for every 100m/330ft of ascent. These time checks are not intended to predetermine your own pace but are meant to be useful reference points. A walk might easily take you *twice as long* if you dawdle over the scenery, nature-watch or stop for the thousand little reasons which bring walkers to a halt.

Our walking **maps** are based on the Tour and Trail map mentioned on page 29, revised only a few months before publication by its designer, Jan Kostura, who also checked most of the walks at the same time.

Walking safely depends in great part on *knowing what to expect and being properly equipped*. For this reason we urge you to read through the *whole* walk description at your leisure *before* setting out, so that you have a mental picture of each stage of the route and the landmarks. One or two walks are waymarked, but **waymarks** may be found along parts of the others. *Only follow waymarks if they are confirmed by the route description.*

Free **GPS track** downloads are available for all the walks in this book: see the *Walk & eat Rhodes* page on the Sunflower website. *Even if you don't use GPS* on the ground, you could use the track downloads to preview the walks in advance.

Thunderstorms in late autumn, after a long summer drought, can cause **flash flooding**, potentially a serious danger to walkers. Keep an eye on the forecast at this time of the year and do not take risks with the weather.

ON ARRIVAL
Tourist information

The main **tourist office** (EOT) is in Rhodes Town, at the corner of Makariou and Papagou [1 on the plan inside the front cover]. Ask for the following; they are all free: bus timetables; opening hours/admission prices (for archaeological sites and other attractions); timetables for boat trips to various islands; map of the island (including a map of the Old Town and a list of useful telephone numbers).

An excellent **map of the island** is the 1:50,000 Tour and Trail map published in 2022 by Discovery Walking Guides.

Transport

There is a very good **bus service** on Rhodes, both within the city and out to surrounding towns and villages. There are frequent services out of Rhodes Town to popular destinations like Faliráki and Líndos, but this changes according to demand. Regularly updated timetables are available from the tourist office or key in 'Rhodes bus timetables in English'. KTEL buses cover the east of the island, Roda buses the west.

Taxis are easily found in Rhodes Town and most other tourist centres. When three or four people are sharing, they can be reasonably cheap and a more convenient option than the bus. Most taxi drivers on Rhodes speak English, so you should be able to establish the fare before setting out — or make sure the journey is being metered.

Shopping for self-catering

Most self-catering accommodation on Rhodes is limited to facilities for throwing breakfast together. There are usually two hot plates combined with a fridge unit, and cooking utensils are minimal. There was a time — very recently — when we calculated that it was better value to eat out than buy food to cook yourself. It may not hold true now, but it's not so much more expensive to dine out in a taverna.

Few people want to waste warm evenings cooking when they could be out enjoying the atmosphere. There are one or

Street-trader with bread rings (kouloúria)

two meals which can be assembled quickly without toiling in the heat. Salads are easy enough to put together, and most supermarkets have a **vegetable** section of some kind. Larger supermarkets offer a better choice of fresh vegetables — as do the local outdoor markets. Lettuce, tomatoes, onions, cucumbers and peppers are basics which most supermarkets stock. Remember these are often **local produce** and are *not treated or sprayed* in any way to make them look or stay fresh, so they may look a little sad towards the end of the day.

This selection of fresh vegetables is typical of a good Rhodes Town supermarket

Freshly barbecued chicken is also available daily and always a good start for a basic meal. Some of the dips, like *tzatzíki* and *taramasaláta,* can be bought ready-made but, to make your own *tzatzíki*, head for the **delicatessen** counter and buy the strained yoghurt *(filtráro yiaoúrti)* found in a large white plastic drum. Ask for it by weight: we find a half kilo *(misó kiló)* more than enough for two, and it's packed in a plastic container for you. This is the really thick strained yoghurt used by the tavernas to make their own *tzatzíki,* and it is also ideal for yoghurt and

31

honey. (When making any of our recipes back home, be sure to use 'Greek-style' yoghurt!)

The delicatessen counter is where you can buy your **cheese**, too, and there is a much larger selection than just *féta*. Avoid *féta* which has been left on display and allowed to dry out. It loses texture and becomes strongly flavoured. Always buy your *féta* from the drum where it has been kept moist under brine. There are a number of hard cheeses to choose from, including *gravéria*, well worth trying if you like gruyère, and *kaséri*. Soft cheeses are *féta* (readily available in the UK), *kopanistí* and *myzíthra*. Greeks love their *myzíthra*. This is a low-fat cheese rather like a smooth cottage cheese. If you can buy it unsalted (often available in spring), it's great with honey for breakfast, but for the rest of the year it's usually salted.

Meat and **fish** can be bought from the big supermarkets. Except for octopus, squid, tuna and sword-fish steaks, most species of fish on

Supermarket shopping list
washing-up liquid
washing powder for hand
    washing (look for the hand
    wash logo on the box and
    the word *xépi*, the Greek
    word for 'hand')
olive oil soap (excellent for
    removing stubborn stains
    when hand washing)
soap
paper towels and/or napkins
aluminium foil
tissues/toilet paper
scouring pads
salt & pepper
herbs & spices
mineral water
milk
coffee/tea/drinking chocolate
butter
sugar
bread
juice
wine/beer/oúzo
sunflower oil (cooking)
olive oil (salads) & vinegar
eggs
tomato purée
rice/pasta
mayonnaise/mustard

sale may be unfamiliar. In spring and autumn, small fish like whitebait are available, which can be dipped in flour, fried and eaten whole (recipe page 120). Ready-cleaned fish from the freezer offers an easier option for self-catering. Small, ready-made-up *souvláki* (**meat on a spit**) can usually be bought from the meat counter or butchers — handy if you are staying in a complex with a communal barbecue. Similarly, the **sausauge** on Rhodes is packed with meat and another great favourite for the barbecue. All the usual selection of chops and chicken pieces is on offer.

G-F, D-F shopping

People on **dairy-free** diets may have few problems finding staples for their needs in large supermarkets, where soya products may be

Vegetarian, vegan, dairy- and gluten-free recipes

The two books listed below contain straightforward recipes for those with special dietary needs. Both are worth considering if you plan to self-cater in Greece, and are light-weight paperbacks easily packed in your luggage. Both are out of print, but inexpensive copies are available from www.amazon.co.uk.

Greek Vegetarian Cooking by Alkmini Chaitow has plenty of good recipes and menu suggestions. It also indicates which recipes are dairy- and/or gluten-free.

A Vegan Taste of Greece by Linda Majzlik offers plenty of recipes to sample, and a concise, comprehensive listing and description of ingredients. Equally useful for vegetarians and for those on dairy- or gluten-free diets.

Hint: Those with food allergies will find the **Annapolis Inn** on 28th October Street [36 on the town plan] sympathetic to their dietary requirements. Not only are there kitchenettes, but a restaurant with full G-F menu daily.

available. But apart from staples like rice and chick peas, **gluten-free** food has been harder to find, although that has changed in the last few years. Two **health food shops** in Rhodes Town should cater for all requirements admirably — as well as being of interest to **vegetarians** and **vegans**. *To Panéri* [Pavlou Mela 17, ℂ 22410 35877; 29 on the town plan inside the front cover] has an excellent g-f selection — from flours through to ready-made corn bread, pasta, rice cakes, biscuits, and cereals (including organic muesli). English is spoken there too, which is a big help. A second source is *Ktima Mastrosavvaki* [Palaion Patran Germanou 4, ℂ 22410 29450; 30 on the plan]. This shop also stocks a range of vegan, dairy-free and gluten-free products — including the yummy goodies from Schär — and, again, some English is spoken.

Rhodes market

The market used to be held in the Moorish building at Mandráki Harbour, and the old fish market can still be seen in the middle, but the slabs remain empty these days. The main outdoor market [34 on the town plan] is now much larger and lies on the eastern side of town, on Annas Marias Street, next to the main cemetery. Held every Wednesday and Friday, it's a large and colourful affair, with fresh vegetables of every description, fruit, cheese, olives, clothing and just about everything else. Make sure you go in the morning (the earlier the better), as stalls close down rapidly in the afternoon. Fish, poultry and eggs, etc are sold in the shops just across the road. Even if you are not shopping, it's a fascinating snapshot of

Greek culture and the way of life ... and it's hard to believe you will come away without something!

There is a Thursday market [35 on the plan], too, held off Venetokieon Street, due south of the Old Town walls outside the Diágoras football stadium.

A visit to the main market could be incorporated into the walk round the outside of the town walls (Walk 2). We followed narrow Mitropoleos Street from behind Diágoras Stadium straight there. Returning along the coast road (not very riveting initially, but better as you near the Old Town walls), we passed some interesting fish tavernas and

Commercial Harbour

oúzeries. This route also provides a good opportunity to see the Commercial Harbour, where there is often some interesting shipping on view. You can then enter the Old Town through the Marine Gate for more browsing.

This medieval fortress town is the best preserved of its kind in Europe and teems with history and stories around every corner. We never tire of wandering these streets. For more in-depth information it's advisable to consult a general guide book, from which there are many to choose.

rhodes old town
WALK

Start the walk at the north end of **Mandráki Harbour**, using the plan inside the front cover. Developed during the Italian era, Mandráki, with its Italianate buildings and medieval windmills, is the most attractive of the town's three harbours. From the **Church of the Evangelist** [7] on the promenade, almost level with harbour entrance, head in the direction of the old walled town. The harbour entrance is reputed to have been the site of the Colossus of Rhodes, but the more gentle stag and doe emblems of the island now stand watch. Tucked into a corner by the post office [5] is the easily missed **Café People & People** [31; see page 46]. The Turkish-style *Nea Agorá* [6; '**New Market**'] — now a misnomer as the markets have been moved — is mainly given over to tavernas and cafés.

Distance: 5km/3mi; allow half a day

Grade: easy level walking, with limited uphill sections

Transport: 🚌 into Rhodes Town; many buses from outlying areas head for the town in the morning and return in the afternoon. Or taxi to Alexandrias Square, next to the 'New Market'. 🚗 It is almost impossible to park near the centre, except early Sunday morning. There are blue pay-and-display zones, but street parking just outside the centre provides the best opportunity, especially during school holidays. Be prepared to have to walk a little way into the centre.

Refreshments: huge choice; we've selected a few favourites (see pages 46-49)

Opening times/entry fees:
Archaeological Museum & Pythári (next door), one ticket for both €6; 08.30-14.30; cl Monday
Palace of the Grand Masters €6; daily ex Sundays 08.30-15.45
Museum of Decorative Arts €2; 08.30-14.30; cl Mondays
Byzantine Museum (Panagía Kástrou) €2; 08.30-14.30; cl Monday
Note: an economical €10 ticket covers entrance to all the above museums.

37

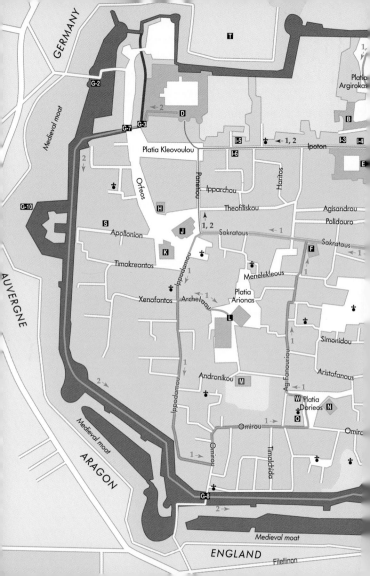

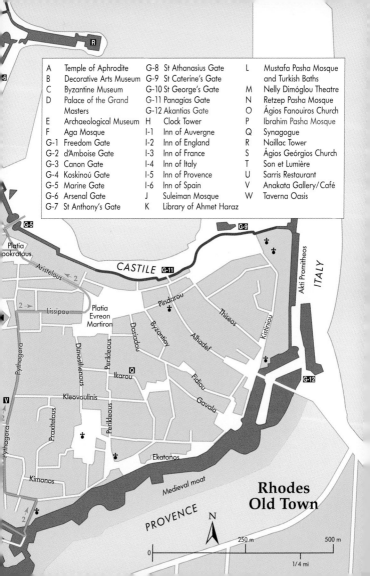

A	Temple of Aphrodite	G-8	St Athanasius Gate
B	Decorative Arts Museum	G-9	St Caterine's Gate
C	Byzantine Museum	G-10	St George's Gate
D	Palace of the Grand Masters	G-11	Panagías Gate
E	Archaeological Museum	G-12	Akantias Gate
F	Aga Mosque	H	Clock Tower
G-1	Freedom Gate	I-1	Inn of Auvergne
G-2	d'Amboise Gate	I-2	Inn of England
G-3	Canon Gate	I-3	Inn of France
G-4	Koskinoú Gate	I-4	Inn of Italy
G-5	Marine Gate	I-5	Inn of Provence
G-6	Arsenal Gate	I-6	Inn of Spain
G-7	St Anthony's Gate	J	Suleiman Mosque
		K	Library of Ahmet Haraz

L	Mustafa Pasha Mosque and Turkish Baths
M	Nelly Dimóglou Theatre
N	Retzep Pasha Mosque
O	Ágios Fanouíros Church
P	Ibrahim Pasha Mosque
Q	Synagogue
R	Naíllac Tower
S	Ágios Geórgios Church
T	Son et Lumière
U	Sarris Restaurant
V	Anakata Gallery/Café
W	Taverna Oasis

Rhodes Old Town

0   250 m   500 m

1/4 mi

The slabs of the old fish market in the centre are now museum pieces (but the toilets beneath are clean and free). An excellent kiosk for fresh *pitas* (pies) is located in the exit onto Alexandrias Square. A walk out past the **windmills** [21] to **Ág Nikólaos lighthouse** [8] allows for a closer view of the yachts and a good overview of the Italian architecture along the waterfront.

Cross **Platia Alexandrias** and continue ahead past sponge-sellers and artists to enter the Old Town, along with the traffic, via Freedom Gate [9; G-1 on the plan on pages 38-39]. The traffic soon hurtles away to the left, as pedestrians enter the **Collachium** (Knights' Quarters). On the left are the remains of a 3rd-century BC **Temple of Aphrodite** [A] then, a little further along, the **Inn of Auvergne** [I-1; 1507]. The building on the right, cloaked in a tumble of bougainvillaea and with a Byzantine baptismal font serving as a fountain, was the first Hospital of the Knights. It was also used by them and later by the Turks as an arsenal. Today it houses the delightful folk art **Museum of Decorative Arts** [B]. Opposite is the Byzantine Church of St Mary, with a chequered history: it was the first Cathedral of the Knights, then converted to a mosque, reconverted to a Christian church, and is now the **Byzantine Museum** [C].

Cobbled Odos Ipoton (Street of the Knights), along which the 'inns' of the various 'tongues' were sited, rises to the right, to the **Palace of the Grand Masters** [D]. From here Walk 2 visits the city walls; see page 43. The impressive building just beyond Odos Ipoton, also on the right, was the new Hospital of the Knights. It now serves as the **Archaeological Museum** [E] and is worth more than a glance. Inside is the Marine Venus, a statue of Aphrodite which inspired Lawrence Durrell's book *Reflections on a Marine Venus.*

Ahead now is the more colourful bustle of Sokratous Street with its old Turkish bazaar atmosphere. A left leads towards the Commercial Harbour and the Jewish Quarter, both of which can be explored on Walk 2. Heading right, you pass projecting

Entrance to the Palace of the Grand Masters. The Knights Hospitallers of St John was founded as a nursing order in the 11th century by Italian merchants, to care for Christian pilgrims en route to Jerusalem. They survived on Rhodes for 500 years before the Turks drove them away. The Knights were divided into seven 'tongues' *(langues)*: France, Provence, Auvergne, Spain, Italy, Germany and England, under a Grand Master whom they elected. Later seven became eight when Spain was subdivided into Aragon and Castile. Each tongue operated from its own headquarters or 'inn'.

wooden balconies, intriguing peaceful alleyways and, on the right, a traditional Turkish tea house. Hidden by an arch of the **Aga Mosque** [F], which juts into the street, the Suleiman Mosque, complete with recently restored minaret, dominates the view ahead. Beyond the mosque there are choices to be made. To the right leads to the Palace of the Grand Masters (another chance to get to the start of Walk 2) and the top end of Odos Ipoton, while ahead is *To Roli* [the **Clock Tower**; H] and **d'Amboise Gate** [G-2].

Turn left into Ipodamou, where **Suleiman Mosque** [J] is on the right, to pass the Turkish Library of **Ahmet Havuz** [K] on the right. Divert briefly left, by the Alter Ego Summer Restaurant, to the **Mustafa Pasha Mosque** and **Turkish Baths** [L] of the same name in Platia Arionas. Behind the baths is the **Nelly Dimóglou Theatre** [M], the best place to see performances of Greek dancing. Continue along Ipodamou and, before reaching the town walls and passing the St Nicholas Hotel on the left, turn left and wend your way into Omirou.

Pass the end of Fanouriou (on the left), but turn left soon afterwards through an archway, into Platia Dorieos with its domed fountain and the **Retzep Pasha Mosque** [N]. The old Byzantine church of **Ágios Fanoúrios** [O] is masked by **Taverna Oasis** [W; see page 46], where the leafy, shaded tables and peaceful ambience makes for an ideal lunch stop. To complete the walk, go left beyond Taverna Oasis into Fanouriou and turn right. Fanouriou is one of the oldest streets and rises back into Sokratous by the **Aga Mosque** [F].

Buy your ticket at the **Palace of the Grand Masters** [D], then head for the steps leading to the gate onto the walls. With the crowds heading off towards distant horizons, you can enjoy a far more peaceful stroll. Climb the steps and go through small **Canon Gate** [G-3], then along the walled path, to reach the outer walls. The walls were divided between the 'tongues', who were responsible for the defence of their particular section (called 'curtains'). This walk passes along the curtains of Auvergne, Aragon and England — in that order.

The Palace of the Grand Masters sits on the highest part of the Collachium (Knights Quarters) and was built on the probable site of the Sanctuary of Helios, the sun god long associated with Rhodes. The rest of the town, more colourful and less

old town walls

Palace of the Grand Masters, To Roli and Suleiman Mosque, seen from the old walls

austere than the Collachium, was called the Bourg and occupied by the merchants. It's interesting to note the scattering of minarets from the Turkish era, many of which have been and are still undergoing restoration, and to overlook the narrow maze of streets. You also have a fine view over the walls themselves — their actual shape and construction. The moat surrounding the walls was left dry deliberately. The complex structure of the entrance gates, designed to make access almost impossible for invaders, is also best observed from above.

The wall walk ends at **Koskinoú Gate** [G-4]. Descend the steps and stay ahead to a T-junction. Go left (but you may choose to go right) and head right along Pythagora, back into the hub of the Old Town. You pass an **excavated section of Byzantine fortification walls** on the left [V]; then, further along, and also on the left, is the **Ibrahim Pasha Mosque** [P] in pleasant Platanos Square.

See map on pages 38-39

Distance: 4km/2.5mi; allow about 2h; the section atop the walls is about 1.7km/1mi; the rest of the walk is inside the walls.

Grade: easy. Although the wall is unfenced on the inside, it's very wide, with no danger of vertigo — but children should be kept in check. There are steps at the start and end of the wall walk.

Opening times/entry fees: Palace of the Grand Masters €6; daily ex Sundays 08.30-15.45

A right from here along Lisipou leads to **Platia Evreon Martiron**, the square of the Jewish Martyrs, with its fountain of bronze sea horses. The square was renamed in memory of the remaining Jewish population who were deported to German concentration camps from that spot in 1943. Continue along Aristotelous, through Platia Ipokratous into Ermou and the **Gate of Thálasini** [**Marine Gate**; G-5]. Venture out through the gates here to see the **Commercial Harbour,** where cruise liners and the ocean-going yachts of the rich and famous dock. Further along to the right is the quieter **Akándia Port**. Return through the medieval gateway and follow Sokratous a short distance to Platia Evdimou and **Sarris Taverna** [U; see page 48], after which a right turn leads back to **Freedom Gate** and exit close to **Platia Alexandrias**.

People & People

Tucked into a corner next to the post office at a busy T-junction, this café is *not* a tourist venue, but very popular with the locals. Drinks are reasonably priced but the tempting snacks more pricey. Good place to sit and watch the world go by.

PEOPLE & PEOPLE CAFÉ
25th Martirou €€

In summer, a *frappé* goes down well, and in the food stakes there is a choice of *pitas* (small savoury pies), sandwiches and *bougátza* (chocolate muffins), chocolate mousse or ice creams

---

restaurants

eat

Taverna Oasis

This really is an oasis within the teaming maze of narrow streets in Old Rhodes Town. By the time you reach here you'll be more than ready to relax in the somnolent surroundings of Platia Dorieos. The wide-ranging, moderately priced menu comes with an English translation of Greek specialities and lists ingredients. The

Some starters: cheese dip, stuffed peppers and black olive paste at the Varkarola Taverna (see page 51)

owner honestly told us that the *kalámari* was frozen, but it was the tenderest frozen *kalámari* we've ever had (see more about *kalámari* on page 12).

Around the corner from Oasis, on Odos Fanouriou, is the pleasant **Nísiros Taverna** in a walled garden setting. We haven't eaten there, but there is an abundance of similar

TAVERNA OASIS
Platia Dorieos (2241 034253
daily, 'morning, noon and night', at
least in the season €€

try the excellent **Greek salad** of lettuce, tomatoes, peppers, cucumber, olives and *féta* cheese, followed by fried *kalámari* and chips *(patátes tiganetés)* — all washed down with the excellent white house wine. Their *kalámari* is shown on page 83.

tavernas within the Old Town walls, all with similar menus. Some are frankly rip-off joints (as we found to our cost). Watch out for comments like 'If you don't like the food you will only pay for the wine': you will find that the price of the wine alone — even house wine in a jug — is astronomical. *Always check prices before you order.* Most establishments are moderate in price, especially the more off the beaten tourist route you go.

One of the management's photos of Sarris: 'romantic atmosphere'...

SARRIS TAVERNA
Evdimou, 18 (corner of Socratous)
Old Rhodes Town (2241 05515
from 09.00 to 23.45 €€-€€€

some menu highlights:

snails and mussels served in a variety of ways

cockles, Sími shrimps, baby shrimps in garlic sauce, marinated **octopus** — and even a delectable speciality **sea urchin** salad (axionó saláta; sea urchins are a special treat in Greece)

ample **steak and meat** dishes

plenty of **Greek specialities**, like soutzoukákia (spicy meat rolls)

Sarris Taverna

Close to the hub of movement through the Old Town, but tucked to one side of quieter Platia Evdimou, Sarris has an extensive Greek and international menu. Snacks and drinks are also available outside main meal times, and their *frappé* is one of the best we've enjoyed on Rhodes.

Here's a chance to really go to town and try something different from the usual taverna fare. How about *saligária yiáxni* (snails in tomato sauce) — or you can just have them with garlic butter if you prefer. Dishes range in price downwards from the expensive to very reasonable, so your wallet doesn't need to be hurt too much.

restaurants

eat

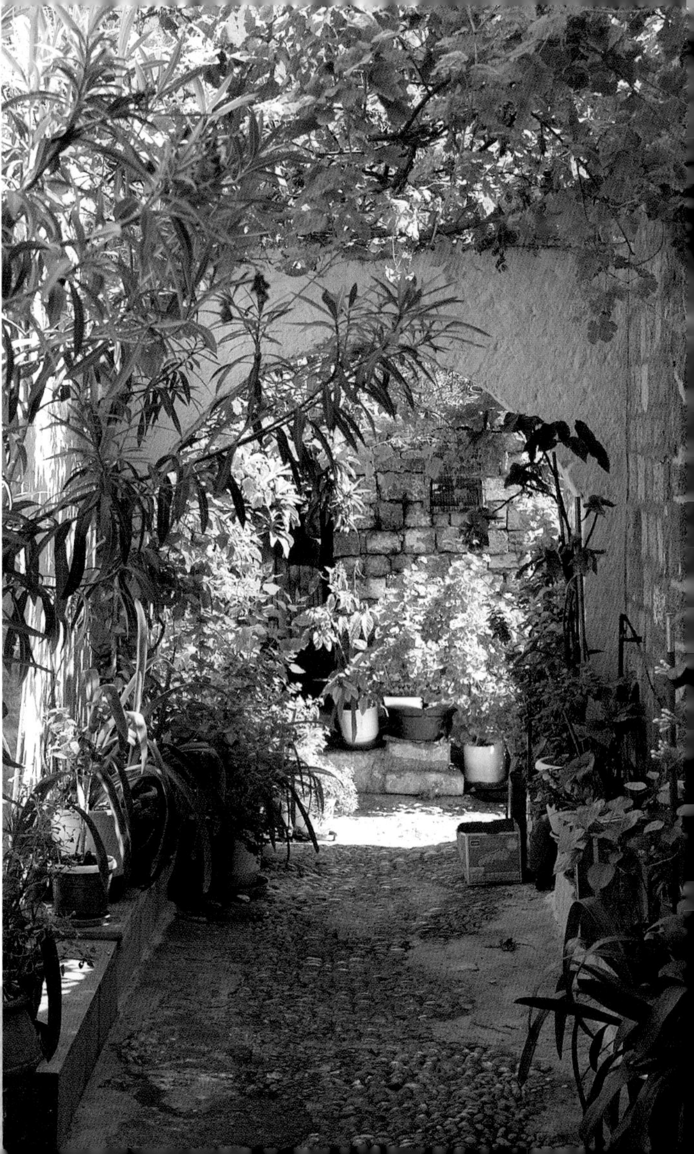

Alley, Rhodes Town

There are many pleasant tavernas you could choose from just outside Rhodes Town, but the three mentioned here are places we particularly like; they are all easy places to stop after a day out, and especially enjoyable for Grecophiles.

Varkarola Restaurant (part of the Amathus Elite Suites complex)

Tucked into the hillside at Ixiá, the Elite Suites (www.elitesuites rhodes.com) is part of the Cyprus-based Amathus Hotel group of five-star hotels offering a high level of comfort and amenities. Within easy distance of Rhodes Town and the airport, it makes a good venue for weddings, conferences, family get-togethers and holidays. The icing on the cake is the excellent level of catering generally (with special attention to dietary needs), and an evening meal at the hotel's Varkarola Taverna is a special treat.

The Varkarola is a relaxing place to be for that special evening meal or light lunch and is open to the general public. There is no need to book for lunch, but evening bookings are essential.

We have spent time here on two occasions and enjoyed both the Friday night Lobster Evening and Tuesday's Greek Evening in the hotel, with food and dancing. The Varkarola is accessible from the beach via a tunnel under the road, for those wishing to call in for lunch. The beach stretches all the way from Rhodes Town to Triánda, so covers a wide-ranging catchment area. Taxis are cheap and easily available for those visiting in the evening.

A selection from the evening menu is shown opposite; there is a lighter lunch-time selection. A good choice of wines is on offer but our favourite, especially with fish, is the white Geravassaliou from Thessaloníki.

restaurants

eat

VARKAROLA RESTAURANT
Amathus Elite Suites
(2241 089900 (hotel reception)
breakfast 07.00-10.15, lunch 12.00-15.00 and dinner 20.00-22.00; all meals à la carte €€-€€€

just a few dishes from the evening menu when we last visited:

appetizers — carpaccio of salmon and sea bass; smoked fillet of duck

salads — 'imperial' salad: smoked salmon and halibut, with caviar, cottage cheese and rocket

main courses — breast of pheasant, flambéd with Grand Marnier, and lemon grass sauce; fillet of monkfish with curry sauce and coconut milk; various pork and lamb dishes

good choice of **desserts**, including their brilliant chocolate soufflé with sauce anglaise (see recipé on page 55)

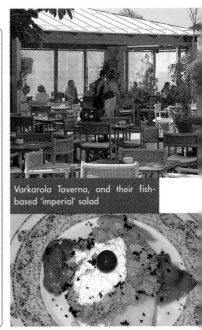

Varkarola Taverna, and their fish-based 'imperial' salad

There was a surprise in store for us when we asked for a recipe at the Varkarola. It was a delicious, mouth-watering hot chocolate soufflé. The restaurant was delighted with our interest, and we were invited to meet the chef the following day for a demonstration. Unfortunately, that did not include another taste of the soufflés, since they need to be chilled for several hours before cooking. We have the recipe for you on page 55. It's so easy to prepare that we now make it on a regular basis when entertaining friends.

Yiannis Taverna

A Greek taverna in the atmospheric, narrow streets of Koskinoú, with eating areas both inside and out. Choose from an extensive menu after first looking round the kitchen to see what they're cooking. Located on the main village street, just south of the church.

YIANNIS TAVERNA
main street, Koskinoú €€

Some different dishes include:
spetzofáï (sausage & peppers in spicy sauce)
seftaliá (homemade sausage)
kondosoúvli (spiced pork on the *soúvla* or spit)
There is also pork in wine, goat, *kokkinistó*, squid and octopus, etc.
good **house wine** in a jug

Before going to Yiannis to eat, it's worth having a look at the 'Traditional House of Koskinoú' — just a few doors from Yiannis, on the same side of the road (open 10.00-13.00 and 18.00-20.00; cl weekends; entrance is free).

restaurants

eat

Profítis Ámos

Don't be put off by the fact that it's in Faliráki; this really is an unexpected haven, far away from the bustle of Faliráki centre. This taverna, a warm-weather-only venue, is on the site of an old monastery complex dedicated to the Prophet Amos. You can sit outside on a terrace tucked into the hillside with an elevated view over the surrounding countryside. Jan ate here twice when checking the walks, 'delicious food, great atmosphere'.

To find it, turn seawards at the staggered junction traffic lights on the southern edge of Faliráki (opposite the road inland to Kalithiés). Fork right immediately, then take the second right (which may have a signpost to Moní Ámos). Stay on this road as it leads towards the hillside and the taverna at the end.

PROFITIS AMOS
Faliráki (6942 775601
summer only, 09.00-24.00 €€

good selection of **mezés, grills** and **vegetarian dishes**

good **white house wine**

When we last visited, the cheerful chef at Profítis Ámos insisted that Eileen had her photo taken with the octopus he was soon to barbecue.

Briám (Baked vegetables)

A popular dish on taverna menus, *briám* is akin to a baked ratatouille, a vegetable dish of mainly potato, courgette and aubergine — with additions to taste. Our recipe is easy, but to make a traditional *briám*, layer the vegetables (see below).

Place the vegetables and peppers in a baking dish. Mix together all the other ingredients and pour over. Cover and bake at 180° C/ gas mark 4 for 1 hour or more.

Layered version: Slice all the vegetables, even the garlic. Start with all the potato layered on the bottom, then the other vegetables, separately, beginning with half the onion. Sprinkle salt, pepper, some garlic, herbs and a drizzle of olive oil over each layer. Finish with a tomato layer; pour over 150 ml stock; Season again to taste. Cover and bake at 190° C/gas mark 5 for about 1 h 15 min. Add extra water if needed.

Optional: Crumble *féta* cheese over the top 20 min before the dish is ready, but cut down the salt in the main dish, as *féta* is quite salty on its own.

Ingredients (for 4 people)

2 large aubergines, in chunks
2 large courgettes, in chunks
3 medium potatoes, cubed
1 green pepper, sliced
1 red pepper, sliced
1 or 2 sticks celery, in chunks
1 medium onion, chopped
2 garlic cloves, crushed
125 ml olive oil
125 ml stock (or water)
4 large tomatoes, skinned & chopped (or 1 tin chopped)
1 tsp oregano
1 tbsp fresh parsley, chopped
salt & pepper

recipes

eat

Poltós eliás mávri (Black olive paste), *illustrated on page 47*

Although this paste, dating from ancient times, may be served as a *mezé* at the start of meals at the Amathus Elite Suites, this recipe isn't from the hotel. Delicious with bread (instead of butter), at the start of a meal or for breakfast. Very easy to make.

Whizz together in a food processor 200 g pitted black olives, 2 garlic cloves, 1 tbsp oregano (or coriander, thyme or cumin), 2 tbsp fresh lemon juice, and 4 tbsp olive oil — until you have a paste. Will store in the fridge for a few days — or pack in small quantities and freeze.

Chocolate soufflé pudding

Have ready 6 crème caramel or small pudding basins (175 ml size), lightly greased and dusted with the cocoa powder.

Beat together the butter and sugar, then beat in the eggs. Melt the chocolate, gently, either over a pan of hot water or on low in the microwave. Add to the above mixture and continue mixing well together. Slowly mix in the vanilla essence and flour and continue mixing until everything is well blended.

Use a spoon or icing bag to fill each basin 2/3 full. Cover and refrigerate for at least 3 h or overnight (the mixture will freeze for 10 days). Bake at 180° C/gas mark 4 for 8-9 min; serve immediately with cream, yoghurt or ice cream.

Ingredients (for 6 people)

125 g butter
100 g icing sugar
4 eggs
cocoa powder for dusting the pudding basins
125 g dark chocolate (70%+ cocoa solids)
two drops vanilla essence
65 g plain flour

Hoirinó kai manitária me lemóni
(Pork and mushrooms with lemon)

Coat the meat in flour and fry in oil with the salt, pepper and cumin. Add the mushrooms, onion, coriander and basil. Stir in the wine.

Transfer to a casserole and cook, covered, in the oven at 170°C/ gas mark 3 for around 1 h 15 min (checking after about 45 min and adding more liquid — either water or wine — if needed). After 1 h 15 min add the lemon juice and return to the oven for a further 10 min.

Serve with rice, pasta, mashed potatoes or chips.

Ingredients (for 4 people)
700 g lean pork in 2.5cm cubes
200 g mushrooms (sliced)
2 large onions
2 tsp dried basil
2 tsp ground cumin
2 tsp ground coriander
500 ml white wine or chicken
   stock
4 tbsp fresh lemon juice
salt & pepper

recipes

eat

Soutzoukákia
(Spicy meat rolls)

This recipe, which we photographed at Sarris Restaurant, makes 12 *soutzoukákia*, three for each person.

Mix all the ingredients thoroughly in a large bowl, then add enough egg to bind the mixture so that it doesn't crumble. Divide the mixture into 12 balls and roll in the palm of the hand to bind well, then form into sausage shapes.

Lightly flour the sausage shapes and shallow fry in oil until they are brown on the outside and more or less cooked through. Drain on kitchen paper. In the meantime, make the tomato sauce.

Put all the ingredients for the sauce in a pan and bring to the boil. Simmer gently for about 30 min. Add more red wine and/or passata if required.

When the sauce is ready, add the cooked sausages to the pan and heat for 10 min.

Serve with pasta, rice, chips or mashed potatoes — and peas or other green vegetable.

Ingredients (for 4 people)
400 g minced beef
35 g stale breadcrumbs
1 small onion, finely chopped
1 garlic clove, crushed
1 tbsp fresh thyme (1 tsp dried)
1 tbsp fresh oregano (1 tsp dried)
1/4 tsp ground cumin
1 small egg, lightly beaten
salt & pepper

Tomato sauce (easy version)
125 ml sieved tomatoes (passata or small tin of chopped tomatoes)
75 ml red wine (or extra sieved tomato)
2 tbsp olive oil
1 small garlic clove, crushed
1/2 tsp dried oregano
salt & pepper

Petaloúdes — The Valley of the Butterflies — is one of the island's top tourist attractions, so it's unlikely you will find yourself alone in the valley. But many of the organised tours only walk a short way downhill, then it's back to the coach — so the crowds thin quickly. And very few tourists visit Moní Kalópetra up the hill.

petaloúdes

WALK

It's unusual for a butterfly to become a top tourist attraction, and even more unusual when the star attraction is not a butterfly at all — but a colourful moth, the Jersey tiger moth, *Euplagia quadripunctaria*. It's easy to pass dozens of them resting on the dark bark of the trees, but only when yours eyes become accustomed will you realise that there are hundreds of them all around you. And only when they are in flight will you appreciate their colours. The tree which attracts this lovely moth to this particular valley is the liquidamber tree, *Liquidamber orientalis*. Its leaf looks very like the plane tree, *Platanos orientalis*, except much smaller.

During the 'butterfly' season, visitors are requested to refrain from making sudden noises — like clapping — to make them fly. The disturbance caused by noise is one of the reasons the moths are reducing in numbers. Out of season, it's still a

Distance: 3.4km/2.1mi; under 2h

Grade: easy-moderate; an overall height gain of about 200m/650ft (many steps). The entire route is along a path (cobbled in parts). Good shade — beware the tree roots!

Equipment: see page 27

Transport: 🚌 from Rhodes Town to Petaloúdes (summer only): departs from [3] on the town plan at 09.30 and 11.30; returns at 12.30 and 15.30. Or 🚗 car or taxi to the lower entrance at Petaloúdes (limited parking close to Taverna Petaloúdes, (36° 20.394'N, 28° 3.589'E), otherwise park above in the large car park).

Refreshments: Ample refreshment stops during high season: Taverna Petaloúdes at the start; a café/bar at the upper entrance; a snack bar near Moní Kalópetra

Opening times/entry fee: open daily from 08.00 until sunset; entry €3 (mid-Apr to mid-Jun), €5 (mid-Jun to early Sep, when the 'butterflies' are active), €3 Sep to end Oct. Otherwise entry is free. Natural History Museum entry fee €3

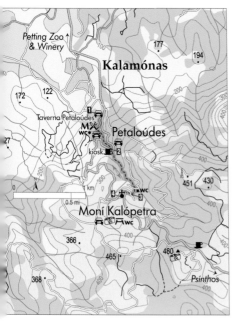

beautiful valley and a worthwhile walk. You may not have the butterflies, but there is more chance of solitude.

The walk starts at the **car park** at the bottom of the valley (**1**). Walk past **Taverna Petaloúdes** and the **Natural History Museum** opposite. Head uphill through the taverna to the entry booth. Keep your entrance ticket to hand, as it will have to be shown each time a pay booth is passed. Just continue uphill on the path through the valley, now under good shade. The 'butterflies' can be quite active in this lower section at the height of the season.

Rise through a pleasant **café area** (**2**) to reach the **road to Psínthos** (**15min**). To the right is a toilet block but go left, briefly, along the road, then head right past a pay booth to continue uphill through the valley. Route-finding isn't a problem as the path heads uphill through the main section of the valley with the opportunity for short diversions. In spring, *Cyclamen* *repandum* is quite abundant and compensates for the lack of 'butterflies'. In fact, this is one of the best places on the island to find it.

After crossing a wide track, you come to a third pay booth and a flat area with seating and more toilets by a **snack bar** (**3**; **40min**). Follow the paved path to the right. Then go left up steps, to the road. Turn left, then go right into the car park at **Moní Kalópetra** (**4**; **50min**).

Below: *Cyclamen repandum* and a Jersey tiger moth

Return by the same route, downhill this time, back to **Taverna Petaloúdes** and the **car park** (**1h30min**).

For those with a car, there is an opportunity to visit the nearby Farma Petting Zoo. Children especially will love this — a lunch of (excellent) ostrich burgers! Finish off with a wine tasting session at the winery, where we particularly enjoyed the red wine; it's close to the access road to the Petting Zoo.

Taverna Petaloúdes

This café, at the start and end of the walk, is extremely welcoming. It prides itself on using extra virgin olive oil from its own olive groves and fresh, locally-sourced produce.

TAVERNA PETALOUDES
at Petaloúdes, oppsite the museum
butterfliesrestaurant.gr €€
open when the valley is open

specialities are moussaka and various pasta dishes, prepared in their wood oven in traditional style

Taverna Petaloudes, a welcoming oasis by the stream, has been open since 1948.

Taverna Pigí Fasoúli

Most visitors only get as far as the cluster of tavernas in Psínthos square, but this was a particularly special find for us. Great for those in search of genuine Greek food, with an extensive menu, very reasonable prices and a quieter location. Pigí Fasoúli (rated 4.7 out of 5 on Trip Advisor in 2021) lies downhill to the left, a short way along the road from Psínthos to Archípoli. Better still, park in Psínthos square and take this delightful six-minute riverside stroll to the taverna (see opposite).

TAVERNA PIGI FASOULI
Psínthos/Archípoli road €€
www.pigifasouli.gr

the speciality is **sikotariá** (fried pieces of liver and kidney) — it is really, really tasty, *but not shown on the menu!*

also tempting here are **loukániko** (lean and tasty village sausage), **pitaroúdia** (recipe page 62), **kolokithákia** (recipe page 105) and a house speciality dessert, **talagoútes** (recipe page 67)

restaurants

eat

From the square go roughly east, to the Petaloúdes road junction on the left. To the right is the hollow, stunted trunk of a once-majestic *Platanos* (plane) tree. Go down the steps here to a fountain area, then keep right and cross the river on stepping stones. Go left, downstream, along the very pleasant and shaded, cobbled path beside the river, which is now on your left. The path crosses back over the river before reaching the plane-shaded *platia* and fountain below the taverna, across the river to your right.

Walk back the same way or, from Pigí Fasoúli, follow the road to the right, then keep right when you come to the Archípoli road, back to the square in Psínthos.

Farma of Rhodes Petting Zoo

After visiting Petaloúdes, this is a quiet place to wander around, away from the tourist bustle, before you have lunch. The farm nestles in the countryside just over 1km along a road leading left off the Kalamónas/Petaloúdes road. This road is just before the winery of Anastasia Triandáfillou (also on the left), around 1.6km/1mi from Petaloúdes.

Besides plenty of ostriches (the farm raises around 200 a year), there is a donkey, a llama, animals and birds from Asia, Australia and India, and a few fallow deer. In Greek, the male deer is *elefós,* the female *elafína,* and the plural *eláfia.* The deer are very shy creatures and at one time were thought to be extinct, but we actually encountered a mother and baby once while out walking.

The café/restaurant, with adjacent children's playground and souvenir shop, sits in an elevated position, with good views over the surround-

> **FARMA OF RHODES PETTING ZOO**
> signed off the Kalamónas/Petaloúdes road
> (6945 327 142; www.farma-rhodes.com
> open daily all year; admission €10 (children
> 3-12 years €7; restaurant/café €€
>
> the speciality is **ostrich meat** (fillet steaks,
> burgers, schnitzel and omelettes)
>
> also Greek mezés, salads (including Greek),
> sandwiches, pizzas, crèpes and ice cream
>
> **stifádo** (veal and shallot stew) and
> **revíthia** (a village stew of meat, chickpeas,
> tomatoes and onions cooked in the oven)
> are also available in the cooler months
>
> wine, beer, soft drinks

A juicy ostrich burger — not just for kids

ing countryside. It's a restful place for a cup of coffee, oúzo and mezédes or a light lunch.

Ostrich meat is low in cholesterol, so it's a healthy lunch option. Try the juicy ostrich burgers or really go for it and have an ostrich schnitzel. If you aren't keen on burgers because of the bun, ask for a burger, minus the bun, and have it with a salad. The meaty burger here is very moist and delicious. The ostrich omelettes are lovely and light; unbelievably, an ostrich can lay an egg every two days, and one ostrich egg makes eight omelettes!

Anastasia Triandáfillou Winery

Near the Ostrich Farm and Petaloúdes, this small organic winery produces a limited number of high-quality wines. The grapes, locally grown, include the white *Athíri* and red *Mandilári*.

Although production is on a limited scale, the wines are quite gluggable and reasonably priced. A visit to taste the wine after the petting zoo makes a fitting end to a full day.

Open daily all year round from 09.00-19.00, they also sell local honey. Their website is at www.estateanastasia.com.

Revíthia sto horiátiki foúrno (Chickpea stew)

Dust the meat in seasoned flour and brown in the olive oil, then set aside.

Soften the onion and garlic in the pan. Stir in the tomato paste, dried oregano, chopped tomato and salt & pepper. Bring to the boil, then add the browned meat.

Re-heat and add extra water if needed. Place in a casserole and cook at 170° C/gas mark 3 for about 1 h.

Remove the casserole from the oven and stir in the chickpeas, then return to the oven for a further 20 min.

Hint: This recipe also works well in a wine-based sauce with pork. Omit the tin of tomatoes and replace with 200 ml of white wine. Add 1 tbsp flour mixed with white wine when the chickpeas are added.

Ingredients (for 4 people)

400 g cooked chickpeas (or 2 x 425 g tins, drained)
1 kg cubed pork or beef
2 medium onions, chopped
2 garlic cloves, crushed
2 x 400 g tins chopped tomatoes
2 tbsp tomato paste
250 ml stock (chicken or beef) — or wine
1 tsp dried oregano
3 tbsp fresh parsley, chopped
1 heaped tsp cumin (optional)
4 tbsp olive oil
salt & pepper

recipes

eat

Pitaroúdia (Chickpea cakes)

Either reconstitute dried chickpeas in cold water for 24 hours, then drain, or use the same quantity of tinned chickpeas. Mash or process the chickpeas, almost to a paste, and mix with the onion, tomato, mint and flour. Season with salt & pepper to taste.

Add just enough liquid to bind together. Shape the mixture into thin round cakes about 7 cm in diameter. Dust with flour and fry in hot sunflower oil (see notes on page 10) on both sides until golden brown.

Hints: Not all *pitaroúdia* contain tomato or courgette. Make sure your version is well seasoned, or they may taste bland. For a spicy version add 1 tsp cumin or curry powder. Another tasty alternative is to use 1 large boiled potato (preferably cooked in its skin before peeling and mashing) in place of the flour — a good use for left-over mashed potato.

Pitaroúdia as we serve them at home

Ingredients (for about 12 cakes)
400 g chickpeas or (2 tins drained weight)
1 large onion, grated
1 large ripe tomato, peeled, deseeded & chopped
  and/or a grated courgette (optional)
1 tbsp fresh mint or dill, parsley etc, chopped
50 g flour
salt & pepper
1 small egg or a drop of water to bind
  together (add a little at a time)

recipes

eat

Talagoútes (Pancakes with honey and nuts)

These are basically a small thick pancake topped with honey and nuts, more like a drop scone in size and slightly thicker.

Make the batter by mixing the flour, baking powder and salt. Break the eggs into a hollow in the centre of the flour and gradually mix together, with a little milk if needed, to make a thick batter. The mixture shouldn't spread too much when dropped into the pan. Beat well and leave to stand for a while.

Heat some unsalted butter or light cooking oil in a frying pan. Drop 1 tbsp of the mixture into the pan for each pancake. Cook 2 min, then flip over and cook a further 2 min. Be careful not to cook these thick pancakes at too high a temperature, or they will burn.

Place on a plate and pour over runny honey, then sprinkle with toasted sesame seeds or chopped walnuts. Serve topped with a blob of ice cream or cream.

Suggestion: To make fruity pancakes, add 25 g of sugar to the mix, then fold 125 g of blueberries or raspberries into the batter just before cooking.

Ingredients (for 8 servings)
75 g plain flour
1 tsp baking powder
1/4 tsp salt
2 eggs
milk — a little, to make a
    thick batter
unsalted butter or light oil

Trickling streams, rustic bridges, the scent of pine, a taverna, and a lake feeding seven springs — that's Eftá Pigís. (By the way, all the signs read 'Epta Piges', but we spell it differently to aid pronunciation.) Since this is one of the island's top touristic sights, *arrive early* if you're driving — or you may find the car parks full.

eftá pigís ('seven springs')

WALK

Start the walk at the **car park** at **Eftá Pigís** (**1**). Walk to the right of the taverna and to the left of a toilet block. Behind the taverna, by signposts, turn right for 'Tunnel, Lake'. You pass the **western entrance to the tunnel** (**2**) and continue along a pleasant woodland path on the eastern bank of the stream. The remains of an **old watermill** (**3**) come into sight on the left and a **rock overhang/cave** on the right. Then you reach the main Archípoli/Kolímbia road with its **bus stop** (**4**) and main entrance to the springs.

Turn right on the road and about 40m/yds before a concrete wall ahead, turn right on another pretty woodland path marked with a red dot. The path climbs on the right side of a stream, initially beside a rock face, and edges a **painted cross** on the right. You pass the remains of an old bridge and continue south along the

Distance: 6km/3.7mi; 2h15min

Grade: easy-moderate, with one short steep, awkward section; overall height gain of 150m/380ft

Equipment: see page 27

Transport: 🚌 to Eftá Pigís (departures from [2] on the plan; daily at 10.30 and 12.00; returns at 14.00 and 17.00); pick up the walk at **4**. Or 🚗 car or taxi to the main car park at Eftá Pigís (36° 15.193'N, 28° 6.857'E).

Refreshments: Eftá Pigís taverna

Longer walk: Eftá Pigís circuit from Archángelos. 11.3km/7mi; 3h30min. Grade as main walk; mostly along tracks to Eftá Pigís. 🚌 to Archángelos (Rhodes/Lindos bus, departures from [2] on the plan; very frequent in the main season). Or 🚗 car or taxi to Archángelos (alight/park near the bridge over the river on entering Archángelos from Rhodes Town (36° 12.932'N, 28° 7.055'E). From the bus stop, head north over the bridge **15** towards Rhodes Town and, almost at once, take the first road left (inland). Refer to the map to walk to Eftá Pigís (on straightforward tracks). Follow the main walk from **1** to **13**, then continue back to Archángelos by again referring to the map.

path. Then turn up left before some boulders and climb a steep bank, where you might need to use your hands — the only awkward climb in the walk, and it doesn't last long.

You emerge on a water-course, where you continue alongside this canal, between giant boulders. A '**waterfall**' (**5**) marks the start of the canal — the falls come over the concrete wall of a dam. Take stone steps up to the right, pass the dam wall and continue beside the 'lake' — which *may* be almost dry, although at times it's deep enough for swimming. Now the path passes the **easterly tunnel entrance** (**6**). People *do* paddle through, but it is dark, low, wet, and potentially dan-

Savas Pottery

If you are travelling to Archán-gelos by car, a pleasant diversion is to follow the old national road which forks off right 1.6km/1mi south of the Kolímbia junction. This short stretch of road (only around 3km/2mi) passes through rural countryside. Around 1km before rejoining the main road at Archángelos, watch for the white buildings of Savas on the left. This lovely traditional pottery is open every day in season and Tuesday and Friday afternoons at quieter times. If pottery is your 'thing', call 6936607152 or 2244 022292/023361 to see if the pottery will be open and if there may be any hands-on pottery-making demon-strations in the offing. Past Savas, a left turn at the main road and then a right turn leads to the start of Alternative walk 4 and Walk 5 in Archángelos.

gerous — we don't recommend it. Instead, take the path above the tunnel, to emerge at the end of the taverna terrace.

Then cross a bridge and follow the path to the left, initially alongside the **Seven Springs** (**7**), to rise into the pine trees — some of which you may have to duck under or clamber over.

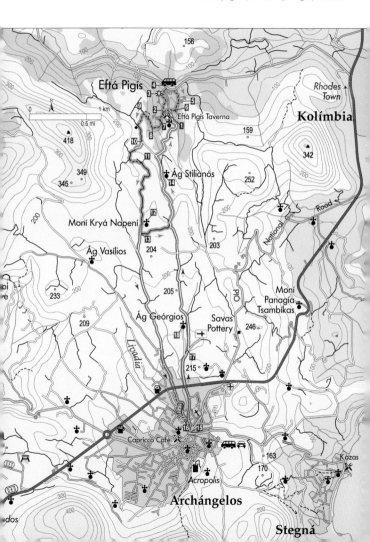

Eftá Pigís

Rhodes Town

Kolímbia

156

159

Eftá Pigís Taverna

418

342

349
345

Ág Stiliános

252

Moní Kryá Napení

204

203

Ág Vasílios

233

National Road

205

209

Ág Geórgios

Savas Pottery

246

Moní Panagía Tsambikás

Livádia

215

Capriccio Café

163

170

Kózas

Acropolis

Archángelos

Stegná

dos

1 km
0.5 mi

The odd red dot on trees show you this is the right path — ignore the 'STOP' sign! Just 250m/yds from the 'STOP' sign, the *path turns sharp right* (**8**) and you reach a track in a tiny olive grove, *still in the midst of the pines.* Terraces open up on your left soon after. Be sure to keep left before the end of this olive grove, to follow a path rising over these shallow terraces (do *not* follow the track!).

You rise into a large area of **olive groves** (**9**). Here you have reached the fenced corner of a farm. Turn left, to keep beside the fence and, a minute later, look for a track running parallel to the fence. You reach it at a white farmhouse; follow it left between the fences of two farms. Beyond a concrete section of track (where it crosses a stream), turn right (**10**) on a narrow dirt track, in front of another fence. Head for a long low hill. In under three minutes, almost at the end of the hill, you pass a **concrete trough** on the left dated 1996. Continue round the base of the hill. *Then watch out:* you pass between two rocks and, 40m/yds further on, *be sure to* fork left uphill on a faint path.

After 100m you rise onto a track, opposite a **concrete hut** (**11**; **2h10min**). Turn right; then keep to this track as it follows the valley into a U-bend to the right. The valley eventually reduces to a gully, and the track — momentarily a paved lane — continues past red-domed **Moní Kyrá Napení** (**12**; **1h**); its main gate is usually locked. Just under 100m from the *moní*, where the compound fence ends, fork left on a good track (**13**). *But for the Alternative walk keep straight on.*

Keep left as you join a tarmac lane, with a sign for 'Epta Piges'. But the tarmac lane becomes a dirt track at an orchard,

Moní Kyrá Napení

with its entrance gate on the left. You pass the small **Stilianós chapel** on the right (■; **1h15min**); then, 300m further on, fork right on a track signposted to 'Epta Piges'. This steeply descending track is intermittently concreted. A view of the chapel at Seven Springs opens up after a bend to the left. Come to a T-junction at a fence, and turn left as indicated by three large arrows painted on a wall. After 20m the tarmac gives way to dirt track. You pass the small church just before the tarmac access road back to **Eftá Pigís** (**2h15min**).

Capriccio Café

An amazing discovery, this café certainly lifts its clients a world away from the traditional and invariably ghastly Greek 'nes'. But the prices aren't over the top. Recline on couches by open windows in summer while enjoying an iced drink. To get there from the bridge over the concrete river bed, head 180m southwest along the main street through Archángelos, and the café is near the right-hand corner. Be sure to specify whether you want your drink hot (*zestos*) or cold (*kreeos*).

CAPRICCIO CAFÉ
Archángelos (2244 023333
daily all year €€

huge choice of **chocolate drinks** (classic dark, milk, hazelnut, almond, white, chocolate & coffee, etc), iced teas, *granitas*, ice creams, fondues, cakes and sandwiches …

for **teas** there are various choices like lemon, jasmine, peach, Egyptian flowers … **coffee** lovers will not be disappointed either!

Eftá Pigís Taverna

If lunch in dappled shade accompanied by friendly ducks appeals, then this is the place to be. Open only during the main

EFTA PIGIS TAVERNA
Eftá Pigís, (22410 56259; www.
7springs.gr; open in season from
09.00 till 22.00 €€

premium aged meats a speciality; olive oil from their own groves; fairly extensive typical Greek menu

season, the area is a hive of activity, especially at weekends when it's a popular haunt of the Rhodians themselves. The café above is the place for a snack, while the terrace below, just above the river, attracts the diners.

restaurants

eat

A *saganáki* is a small frying pan, usually with two handles, and the food is served in the pan.

Saganáki (Fried cheese)
not illustrated

Heat butter or light oil in a frying pan until hot. Press the cheese into the flour to coat. Fry in the hot oil for about 1 min each side, until golden brown. Transfer to a warm dish, season with lemon juice and black pepper to taste. Serve immediately.

Tip: Slabs of *haloúmi* cheese (unfloured) can also be grilled. Serve with wedges of lemon.

Féta saganáki sto foúrno
(Baked *féta*)

Place the cheese and pepper slices in an ovenproof dish, and put the tomato slices on top. Add a drizzle of olive oil, sprinkle of oregano and black pepper. Wrap the whole thing in a foil parcel – or use a covered clay pot for the baking. Bake at 180° C/gas mark 4 for 15-20 min.

Ingredients (for 4 people)
250 g hard cheese such as *haloúmi*, cut in 10-15 mm-thick slices
lemon juice (to taste)
black pepper, ground
seasoned flour

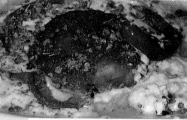

Ingredients (for 4 people)
400 g *féta* cheese, either sliced or crumbled
1 red or green pepper, finely sliced
2 large tomatoes, thinly sliced
olive oil
oregano
black pepper, ground

recipes

eat

This easy route to Stegná Bay offers especially good views over the bay on the descent, while on the short climb back up, you can visit the church of Panagía Epakoúsa and then look up to Archángelos itself — with its castle crown and the wonderful 'wedding cake' church of the Archangel Michael, which gives the town its name.

archángelos — stegná bay circuit

WALK

Start the walk in **Archángelos** at the **bridge** over the concrete river bed (**1**). Walk down the road signposted to Stegná Beach. When the road forks after 175m/yds, keep ahead (right). This road also forks after 250m (**7min**): go left, soon afterwards heading into open countryside where the road reverts to track. At a fork after just under 500m (**2**; **12min**), go left along a gently rising minor track. (Were you to follow the main track at this point for another five minutes you would come to waypoint **9** — ideal for taking a very short circuit including the castle.)

Now stay ahead on this new track and ignore any forks to the left. As the track rises to a **crest** after 650m (**3**; **25min**), fork right downhill on a path. (This turning should be marked by cairns.) Panoramic views over Stegná Bay

Distance: 8.7km/5.4mi; about 3h

Grade: moderate, with an overall ascent of 260m/850ft. Mainly track, apart from the steep, stony descent to Stegná and the climb back up, which demand agility. *Almost no shade*

Equipment: see page 27

Transport: 🚌 or 🚗 as Longer walk 4, page 69

Refreshments: Capriccio Café in Archángelos (see page 74), as well as other cafés and tavernas; selection of cafés and tavernas at Stegná Bay, but don't rely on any being open in Stegná outside the holiday season. Greek friends recommend two tavernas in Archángelos: Savas (📞 2244 023125) and Afentiká (📞 2244 023640); we've not had the opportunity to sample them ourselves.

Alternatives: (1) just walk one way, to Stegná (3km/1.9mi; 1h05min; moderate) and return by taxi or bus (summer-only 🚌 service; check locally); (2) walk to Stegná and then retrace your steps (6.2km/3.9mi; 2h30min; moderate); (3) from Stegná, walk back along the road: Stegná Bay stretches for 1km from the harbour to Kozas Taverna before reaching the road to Archángelos, from where it's another 2.6km/1.6mi; 1h uphill back to the start.

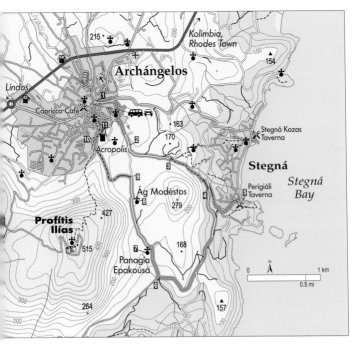

open up as the rocky path descends alongside a gulley on the left. This is an enjoyable route, but some agility is required.

Cross a **stabilised track/new road**; **4**; **55min**) and continue in the same direction through an olive grove. Then head to the back of a **blue and white aparthotel** (Bella Vista). Pass behind the hotel and make your way downhill to the **fishing harbour at Stegná Bay** (**5**; **1h05min**). Our two featured fish tavernas are To Perigiáli, immediately to the right, and Stegná Kozas, which

sits overlooking the shore
1km along the coast road at
the far northern end of the
resort, close to where the road
enters Stegná from Archángelos.

To continue the walk *from
the harbour,* return to waypoint **4** (**1h20min**) and
turn left along the
track/road. Follow this
up to a crest, then
descend to a **T-junction**
(**6**). Turn right, uphill,
on another surfaced
track/road. You reach a
high point (**1h50min**),
from where there are
excellent views of the
coastline and Feraklós
Castle atop a rocky
outcrop. Beneath the
rocky hill ahead is a

Stegná Bay (top) and descending the path
alongside the gulley

small white church, your next landfall. Keep along this road,
ignoring tracks left and right, to reach the modern church of
Panagía Epakoúsa (**7**; **1h55min**), in a strategic position
overlooking the coast. Frescoes adorn the inside walls.

From here fork left inland; the way soon becomes stabilised

Ág Geórgios, a small church inside Archangelos Castle

track once more — with good views to Archángelos and its castle — and over right to Moní Tsambíka. You pass a **shrine (8)** on the right dedicated to Ág Modéstos, one-time Bishop of Jerusalem who died in 634 AD. The shrine is most likely in memory of a local farmer, as the saint was a doctor and guardian of animals whose name day is celebrated on 16th December.

The red-earth track seen ahead to the left of the castle is your eventual route. For now, stay on this main track for another 500m (10 minutes), then take a track off left (**9**; **2h15min**). Rise to pass well to the left of the castle, then descend to a crossing road (**2h30min**). Turn right, soon enjoying fine views over Archángelos. Take the path uphill to the right, then the steps to **Archángelos Castle** (**10**; **2h35min**).

Leave the castle via the same steps at first, but ignore the steps rising from the left used earlier. Head towards the wedding-cake bell-tower and turn left at a T-junction, to take more steps down to a concrete road. Cross straight over and follow a lane diagonally right downhill. After 80m, turn sharp left (back the way you came; **11**) and then bend round to the right, to pass to the right of the church and bell-tower. Descend to a T-junction and turn right to the main road through **Archángelos**. Then turn right again, back to the **bridge** (about **3h**).

STEGNA KOZAS TAVERNA
Stegná (2244 022632; daily in season; in winter only Fri evenings, Sat & Sun €€
www. stegnakozas.gr — look at their menu!

tasters include olive paste with Archángelos village bread

various **salads**: Greek, Italian, Cretan and the local *petroniatíki*

hearty **home-made soups** — more than enough for a light lunch: fish, lobster, vegetarian vegetable

fresh fish in abundance daily — every kinds of fish you can imagine (unless there is no fishing due to storms). ***Rouzetiá***: a 500 g portion of fried fish for two people, served with a special garlic sauce

very extensive **wine and beer list**

pastas of all kinds; **risottos**

delicious **desserts** include *baklavá*, *kataïfi* with ice cream, fresh apple pie, and yoghurt, honey & nuts. Try one of their two special sweets: ***melekoúni*** (also called *pastéli*) are sesame & honey bars, a symbol of fertility, usually made for Greek weddings; ***kserotígana*** (*thiples*) are deep-fried pastry rings/shapes covered in honey, sesame seeds and cinnamon

Kozas Taverna

Once you've sampled the food here you'll want to return time and again, if only to go through as many goodies on the menu as possible. This fish taverna, opened in 1932, is a great favourite of the islanders who flock here at weekends for locally-caught fish. Even if you aren't a fan of fish, there is a huge choice of dishes. Of course sometimes not *every-thing* is on the menu *every* day. There is also a children's menu. Stegná Beach was once known as 'Kozas', which is also the family name of the owner.

restaurants

eat

To Perigiáli Taverna

A delightful find, at the opposite end of Stegná to Kozas Taverna, down by the harbour. The state-of-the-art 5-star toilets alone are worth a visit! Perigiáli, like Kozas, is a fish taverna in an idyllic setting. As well as fresh fish delivered straight from

the sea onto the doorstep, there is a large selection of *mezés*, *perigiáli* special salad, village bread, and the best *kalamári* we've had in a long while. All washed down with an excellent house wine and just the setting to round off a good meal with a *soúma* (the local fire water), which goes well with a coffee.

TO PERIGIALI
Stegná harbour
(2244 023444 €€; www.
perigiali-parathinalos. gr
daily in season, in winter
only Fri evenings, Sat & Sun

restaurants
eat

Petroniatíki salad

We have left quantities to individual taste. The salad is served in a dish for 2 persons. Toss together rocket, cherry tomatoes, chopped cucumber, chopped peppers, chopped or thinly sliced onions, black olives, *féta* cubes, oregano & mint. Top with the mashed flesh of roasted aubergine.

Petroniatiki salad at Kozas; below: *kalamári* at Taverna Oasis in Old Rhodes Town

Kalamári tiganitó
(Fried squid)

Use fresh or frozen squid. Clean if necessary, then dry thoroughly. The tentacles will be separate, but leave small squid *(kalamárakia)* whole and cut large fish into rings (see photograph).

All that is needed is to coat the squid with peppered flour and fry in hot fat for about 3 min, until brown and crispy. *Overcooking toughens the flesh.* Drain on kitchen paper. Serve with lemon.

recipes

eat

Kserotígana (*thiples*) (Deep-fried pastry rings and shapes)

Sift the flour into a bowl. Beat the eggs and add to the flour with the lemon zest and sugar, gradually, to make a stiff dough. Add a drop of water to bind if necessary.

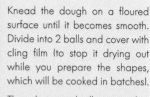

Knead the dough on a floured surface until it becomes smooth. Divide into 2 balls and cover with cling film (to stop it drying out while you prepare the shapes, which will be cooked in batches).

The photograph illustrates that the pastry can be prepared in various ways. You can roll out one of the balls into a long, thin strip; then, using a serrated pastry wheel, trim the edges and cut into 1.5 cm strips. Twist and twirl the strips into rings. Perhaps roll out the other ball and stamp or cut the pastry into various shapes.

Shallow fry in hot oil, 3-5 cm deep, until puffed up and golden brown, turning halfway through. *Beware*: these cook in *seconds* rather than minutes!

Drain on kitchen paper, then serve sprinkled with cinnamon and/or icing sugar, drizzled with honey then topped with chopped walnuts.

<u>Ingredients (for 4 people)</u>
200 g self-raising flour (or use plain flour with 1 tsp of baking powder)
2 eggs
Finely grated zest of 1/2 lemon
10 g caster sugar
100 ml runny honey
chopped walnuts or sesame seeds
cinnamon
icing sugar

Galaktoboúriko (Traditional Greek custard pie)

Custard pie is a popular sweet, with almost as many variations for the basic recipe as there are days in the month.

Prepare a dish or baking tin approximately 18 cm x 18 cm. Line the dish with 6 sheets of filo pastry. Brush each sheet with melted unsalted butter. Leave an overhang of about 4 cm.

Put the semolina, sugar and grated lemon zest (if used) in a saucepan and gradually mix in the milk. Bring to the boil, stirring constantly. Remove the pan from the heat and quickly mix in the beaten eggs. Add the vanilla essence at this stage, if you are using that instead of lemon zest. Pour the lot into the prepared baking vessel.

To make the syrup, slowly dissolve the sugar in a pan with the lemon and water, then bring to the boil. Simmer for 2 min and cool.

Top the custard with another 6 sheets of filo pastry. Tuck under the edges and brush the top with more melted butter. Score the top in a diamond or square pattern (to delineate the servings).

Bake at 180° C/gas mark 4 for 30 min, until golden brown. Then pour the cooled syrup evenly over the top and leave to soak before serving.

Ingredients (for 6 large servings)

12 sheets filo pastry
400 ml milk
60 g semolina
60 g caster sugar (Greek recipes usually call for 70 g)
2 eggs, beaten
unsalted butter, melted
1/2 lemon, finely grated zest (or 1 tsp vanilla essence if preferred)

For the syrup

130 g sugar
75 ml water
juice of 1/2 lemon

Just why this 14th-century Byzantine church is called Saint Nicholas of the Hazelnuts *(Foundoúkli)* is uncertain. The best guess is that hazel trees grew in the surrounding hills at some time in the past. Normally the church is open, so you can see the interesting old frescoes.

foundoúkli circuit

WALK

The walk starts from the church of **Ág Nikólaos Foundoúkli** (**1**); there's a picnic area with tables adjacent to the car park; locals sell fruit, nuts, honey and drinks here in high season. Walk along the road towards Profítis Ilías. After 140m/yds turn right into a smaller road. The field track entering from the right

Distance: 5.3km/3.3mi; 1h45min

Grade: moderate/strenuous, a track walk with overall height loss/gain of 180m/820ft; some agility required

Equipment: see page 27

Transport: car/taxi to St Nicholas Foundoúkli. Park opposite the church (36° 16.456'N, 27° 59.841'E).

Refreshments: café at Profítis Ilías (see Walk 7), tavernas at Apóllona; Taverna Fountoukli en route

almost immediately is used on the return. You pass a **ruin** on the right as the road bends left. At a junction with another **ruin** in the right-hand corner (**2**; **6min**), swing downhill to the right on tarmac. (The stabilised track ahead is the return route.)

Head downhill on this road and, in under 400m from the junction, fork left on a track (**3**). Initially you head downhill, then ascend past olive groves. Rise onto a **ridge** (**25min**), from where there are panoramic views out to the west coast. Sálakos can be seen ahead when the far end of the ridge is reached about 10 minutes later. Start into a descent which is steep and tricky underfoot for a short section where the track is eroded. At a T-junction in a dip (**4**; **40min**), continue downhill to the left. There is more shade now, as the walk enters a more heavily wooded section. Just over 100m along this track, fork sharp left, at first level and then downhill through pines, into the valley. The track curls down for 12 minutes or so, to a stream bed. Cross this, a second stream bed, and then a deeper, wider one (all

Frescoes in Ágios Nikólaos Foundoúkli

three are crossed within a few minutes). This is the halfway point in the walk.

Leave the valley floor on a rough, rising track. It bends left at first, then winds uphill to a T-junction (**5**). Stay left, uphill, and soon enjoy a level section before rising again. You pass a 'log cabin in the woods', **Taverna Fountoukli** (**6**; **1h06min**). It was new on our last visit, and we've not been able to check it out. Continue ahead past the road running downhill to the left on the outward leg (**2**). A little further along, by a **ruin** on the left (where the road you are on swings right to the main road), take the woodland track straight ahead. As this track dips, the red dome of Ág Nikólaos Foundoúkli is seen ahead. Keep ahead in the dip, to rise through the picnic terraces to the car park at **Ág Nikólaos Foundoúkli** (**1h45min**).

Tavernas Fountoukli, Yiarenis and Panorama

Despite not being able to visit **Taverna Fountoukli** because of travel restrictions during the pandemic, we see that it's very popular with visitors, who sing the praises of its setting and the food on sites like Trip Advisor (one reviewer saying that if it snowed in Rhodes she would go to this log cabin every day…). Find their page on Facebook. Disappointingly, they are only open from September to May, and only on weekends.

In that case, drive down to Apóllona, where there is a selection of cafés and tavernas. We suggest taking the signposted road left downhill for 2.6km from the Profítis Ilías road towards Apóllona

FOUNTOUKLI
near Apóllona; surprisingly, this taverna is only open on weekends in winter (from Sep till May) (695 539 6525/695 509 4503 €€
reviews on Trip Advisor say the atmosphere and food are five-star

YIARENIS
Apóllona, open all year from 11.30-19.00 (Fri/Sat/Sun till 23.00) €€
(697 998 5489; tavernayiarenis.gr
traditional Greek recipes; look at the huge menu on their website

PANORAMA
Apóllona, open all year from 08.00 to 16.00, cl Sundays (694 792 3709 €€
typical village food — like *kokkinistó*, *youvétsi*, *sikóti* (liver), meat with potatoes and *mousakás*

and Émbonas. At the first two T-junctions *ignore* the sign-posted left turns to Apóllona. (Turning left too soon, unless you're on foot, leads directly to the back of the village and narrow streets.) On reaching the main road (where a right turn goes to Émbonas), turn left, back towards Apóllona. Soon you will arrive at the entrance to the village and two tavernas facing each other — **Yiarenis**, on the right, and **Panorama** on the left (see the map on page 94).

restaurants

eat

89

Soúpa revíthi (Chickpea soup) *not illustrated*

Fry the onion in the olive oil until softened, then add the garlic. Add the rest of the ingredients and bring to the boil. Cover and simmer for about 15 min, stirring occasionally.

Either leave the chickpeas whole or crush them slightly, add lemon juice and serve with the parsley garnish. (If preferred, you can thicken the soup with 1 tbsp flour mixed with the lemon juice — add this a few minutes before the end of the cooking time.)

Hint: To make this into a main meal, double all the quantities and consider adding your choice of vegetables — perhaps diced carrots, celery, mushrooms, diced courgettes or even broccoli florets.

Serve with bread and a Greek or lettuce *(maruli)* salad (see below).

<u>Ingredients (for 4 people)</u>
400 g dried chickpeas, cooked & skinned (or 2 x 400 g tins, drained)
1 onion, chopped
2 garlic cloves, crushed
2 tbsp olive oil
1 litre stock (chicken or vegetable)
1 tbsp fresh coriander, rosemary or oregano, chopped

<u>*To serve:*</u>
1 tbsp lemon juice
ground black pepper
chopped fresh parsley (garnish)
1/2 tsp cumin (optional)

Marulosaláta (Lettuce salad)

This is a very popular salad, and the herbs (especially dill) and seasoning make it very tasty.

Just cut 1 lettuce into thin strips, add 5 finely chopped spring onions and some finely chopped fresh dill (cubed cucumber can also be used if wished). Mix all these dry ingredients, then add an oil & white wine vinegar or oil & lemon dressing, season with salt and pepper and toss well.

recipes

eat

Kokkinistó (Veal or beef in tomato sauce)

Heat the butter/oil in a frying pan. Coat the meat with seasoned flour and lightly brown in the butter/oil. Add the onions and garlic, then the optional red wine (or water), cinnamon, allspice and tomatoes. Bring to the boil; then either cover the pan with a lid and simmer gently for at least two hours or pour into an ovenproof dish, cover and cook at 170° C/gas mark 3 for about 2 hours — until the meat is tender and falling apart. This is ideal done in a slow cooker at home. Adjust the seasoning according to taste and add extra water, passata or red wine if the mixture appears too dry.

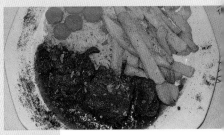

If you include carrots and celery (not Greek, but we like it!), then add more tomatoes to keep up the liquid content. (The number of fresh tomatoes used depends on the size, too — if in doubt, use more.)

Although veal or beef is used in this particular recipe, it can be made with other meat, especially chicken. The Greeks don't usually coat the meat in flour, but we prefer a thicker gravy.

Ingredients (for 4 people — generous portions)

1 kg veal or beef (cut roughly into 3 cm cubes)
100 g butter and/or oil
2 tbsp flour
2 onions, chopped
4 garlic cloves, crushed
50 ml red wine (optional) or water
1/2 tsp cinnamon
1 tsp allspice
4 large ripe tomatoes, peeled and chopped (or 1 x 400 g tin chopped tomatoes)
4 carrots, diced (optional)
2 sticks celery, chopped (optional)
salt & pepper

The charm of this walk lies in the lovely old donkey trail which climbs the hillside easily in long sweeping zigzags. Awaiting you at the top is a woodland circuit via some splendid viewpoints … and then one of the best dishes of locally sourced yoghurt, honey and walnuts that you are likely to find on the island.

profítis ilías from sálakos

WALK

Start the walk in **Sálakos**: leave the *platia* (tavernas, bus stop; **1**) by following the road towards Profítis Ilías. Pass the Hotel Nymph on the left and, as the road bends right, go left along the road signposted as a walking route to Profítis Ilías. After just over 80m/yds, turn right uphill on a stony path with a sign for Profítis Ilías (**2**). An imposing hillside rises ahead, but the climb is much easier than it looks. Soon, there is a fence on your left. At a fork just before reaching a white **shrine** on the right (**15min**), follow the fence

Distance: 8km/5mi; 4h15min
Grade: moderate-strenuous, with a climb/descent of 500m/1640ft; at times quite stony underfoot
Equipment: see page 27
Transport: 🚌 from Rhodes Town to Sálakos (there are a few in season; an early morning bus will allow time for the walk and a late afternoon return). 🚗 to Sálakos; park in the village or drive the first minutes of the walk and park off the lane near waypoint **2** — or under 300m further on, by a shady fountain with benches.
Refreshments: Sálakos tavernas, Elafáki at Profítis Ilías (in season)
Short walk: Circuit from Hotel Eláfos (3km/1.9mi; 1h15min; moderate ascent of 150m/490ft). 🚗 to Hotel Eláfos; make a circuit from **7**.

round to the left, to continue uphill. Negotiate the animal **gate** (**3**), and soon start along the zigzag trail which eases your way up the very steep rock face. Some trees offer welcome shade.

You pass in front of a **water trough** on a left bend (**4**; **30min**). As the trail rises, the views are expansive and provide plenty of excuses to stop. At the **top of the trail**, the now-paved route heads towards the masts on the summit of Profítis Ilías. The trail rises again slightly, to a crossing track (**5**; **1h15min**). The onward route is to the left, but first turn right to **St Michael's church** (**6**; Ag Mixális), a fine viewpoint. The rooftops of the

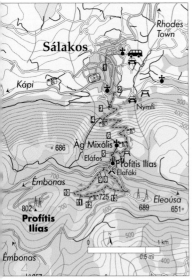

Hotel Eláfos peep above the tree-tops. Back at **5**, continue ahead. Rise below the church of **Profítis Ilías** (**7**) and **Hotel Eláfos**, keep right below the church complex, and then ascend the steps between the church and hotel. **Kafeneon Elafáki (1h35min)** is straight ahead across the main road.

Walk past the café for 50m, then climb stone steps on the left up to **Villa de Vecchi** (Mussolini's mansion; **8**) and then up more steps to his old **chapel** (**9**). Continue on the woodland path (red dots, some cairns). Remains of paving are still visible in places, as you make your way over fallen trees. Go through a **small clearing** and, 35m further on, turn 90° left (**10**). After some shallow steps, the path splits. Go left to a **viewpoint** (**11**) over the way you've come. The paths rejoin after 50m and take you to another **viewpoint** (**12**) on the right — over Eleoúsa and all the way to the Gadoúra Dam. Watch for a large cairn about 10m off to the right of the path; 200m further on, turn right to a third **viewpoint** (**13**).

Back at the junction leading to this last viewpoint, turn right and after about 100m turn sharp left (some 30m before a road). Then, after about 50m, at a junction, ignore the path going left uphill; turn down sharp right and immediately into a hairpin bend to the left. Keep to the left of a ruined house, and you'll come back to 🖪 (**2h50min**). After a yummy yoghurt break at Kafeneon Elafáki, retrace steps down to **Salakos** (**4h15min**).

Kafeneon Elafáki

Set on the wooded slopes of Profítis Ilías, looking down onto Hotel Eláfos, this is a pleasant spot to sit and have a drink and snack. Try the delicious yoghurt shown overleaf.

> **KAFENEON ELAFÁKI**
> **below Profítis Ilías**
> **daily in season; (2246 022280** €€
> various **hot and cold drinks**
> **ice creams**
> *tost* (toasted sandwiches), sandwiches, pizzas, **Greek salad**
> **special:** youhurt, nuts & honey

Salakos tavernas

Most of the tables in the leafy square in Sálakos square belong to **Mixálhs Taverna**; their menu is quite extensive and includes delicacies such as *simiakó* — small sweet shrimps from the island of Sími. But there are a few others in the square to look out for — and prices in these three tavernas are much cheaper than those in more touristy areas.

restaurants

eat

Garídes tiganités (Fried prawns)

For this popular appetizer allow 100-125 g peeled king prawns per person. Coat the prawns in seasoned flour and fry in hot oil (about 5 cm deep), for not much more than 1 min. Drain on kitchen paper and serve with lemon quarters.

Hoirinó tigánia crassáta (Pork in wine sauce)

Coat the pork in the flour and brown in a pan. Remove the meat and set aside. Soften the onion in the pan, then add the oregano, cumin, wine and pork. Bring to the boil.

Reduce to a simmer and cook on a low heat, adding extra liquid (either wine or water) if required — or place in a casserole and cook at 160° C/gas mark 3 for around 1 h 30 min. (We use a slow cooker on low at home, and leave it for a few hours.)

Ingredients (for 4 people)
700 g lean pork, cubed
2 onions, chopped
400 ml white wine

2 tbsp flour, seasoned with salt & pepper
2 tsp oregano
1/2 tsp cumin

recipes

eat

Yoghurt, honey and walnuts (*karídes*), as served at To Elafáki

Yaoúrti me méli kai karïdes
(Yoghurt, walnuts and honey)

A quick and simple desert or snack. Buy the strained yoghurt out of a bulk container, found in larger supermarkets at the cheese and delicatessen counters, by weight (see shopping tips on page 31). Allow 150 g per person.

Stir the yoghurt well and place in individual serving dishes. Top with some honey and chopped walnuts (or your favourite nuts). This is the perfect desert with minimum effort — ideal for self catering!

This walk climbs through a narrow valley to emerge on the Marmári massif — stark limestone terrain populated by sparse holm oaks and a wealth of flora in early spring — including a Rhodian speciality, the red turban buttercup, *Ranunculus asiaticus*. Towards the end of the walk you enjoy an unusual and spectacular view of Líndos.

vlichá to líndos

WALK

Start the walk at the **bus shelter** adjacent to property 613 (**1**): walk 20m/yds back towards Rhodes Town, to a track diagonally opposite (signposted simply 'Rena Sea View Villa' at time of writing). Initially, the track (concreted at the outset) leads inland between wire fencing, into open countryside. Ignore forks to the right and stay with the track as it swings more to the left alongside **goat pens** on the left. A rusting **gravel chute** stands across the shallow gulley on the right, as the rough track heads into a narrow valley. You come to a **gate** across the track (**2**; **14min**); it may be open, but is easily bypassed in any case.

At the point where the track forks right over the

Distance: 6km/3.7mi; 2h20min

Grade: moderate; mainly on paths (waymarked with red dots and cairns) through rocky terrain and with a height gain of 170m/558ft. You must be sure-footed and agile for the descent to Lindos. Almost no shade!

Equipment: see page 27

Transport: 🚌 to Vlichá Bay (Rhodes/Líndos bus, departures from [2] on the plan; very frequent in the main season). Alight at the first bus stop after the Vlichá junction. Travelling by 🚗, drive downhill into Líndos and take the road heading sharp left to the beach (NB: it is easier to go round the roundabout at the bottom, in Líndos Square, and then turn *right* into this road). Park as soon as you can along this road (36° 5.586'N, 28° 5.030E); parking is pay-and-display, but the full-day charge is reasonable. Return to the square for a taxi and ask to be dropped by the bus shelter, 1km before the Vlichá junction. This bus shelter is next to the gates of house no 613.

stream bed (**3**; **20min**), continue ahead on a path towards a cube-like boulder. (Red dots waymark this path further on.) Stay on the path as it weaves between the rocks and rises into a **high pasture** enclosed within the hills (**30min**). The track you

Rhodes Town ↑

Vlichá Bay

Vlichá

Pilónas 226

Lárdos

281

613

Marmári

241

Záta
358

459
Marmári

233

287

378

400

85

Lárdos

Moní Ág Nikólaos

Moní Profítis Ilías

144

141

Péfkos

116

Cape Á
Emiliá

Tomb c
Kleobo

Líndos

Líndos Bay

Memorial

Mythos

Acropolis

Maria's

St Paul's Bay

Arxondiko

Ág Pávlos

62

Cape Soumá

0   1 km
0.5 mi

The path crosses rocky terrain at the top of the escarpment.

left previously crosses the path; keep ahead here, taking the right of two jeep tracks. On your left is a single, huge **spreading Valonian oak** and a **fenced shed** at the base of the escarpment. Goats are cavorting about; their quarters are the caves you can spot in the escarpment up ahead.

Continue by following the red dot-waymarked path towards the right-hand side of the escarpment and locate shallow **steps** hewn out of the rock by the **goat caves** (**4**; under **40min**) — a good place for a break in the shade. The gradient of the route relents as you gradually approach a saddle. On the right (west) is the majestic ridge, peaking in Marmári at 459m/1505ft. Climb the steps to the top of the escarpment and stay ahead as the path briefly skirts some low walls on the right. Red dots and the odd cairn mark the route through the rocky terrain, where **scattered holm oaks (5)** provide the only shade. The flora here is best in early spring, before the rocks get hot in the sun and burn up the annual flowers, bringing their season to an end.

The route heads up the valley, rising above a shallow depression on the right which falls away steeply for a while. Follow the path as it gradually crosses the top end of the depression (**50min**) and heads towards the buttress of rock at the end of the valley on the right. Reaching a high point (**1h**), descend to cross a shallow bowl, heading towards the saddle ahead. The rock buttress is to the right. Reach the **saddle (6; 1h10min)** and pass through a gap in the low wall, to descend through the rocks. Views open up — to the sea and abandoned terraces on the plateau below. The path continues towards the plateau but veers left, gently ascending, before it's reached. Soon, the path skims the **cliff edge (1h20min)** above the Líndos/Péfkos road. Suddenly, the land drops away by a **small saddle (7; 1h35min)**, to reveal a stunning view of Líndos acropolis ahead. The path heads directly towards it.

Now you must be sure-footed and agile for the descent. Follow the skiddy path carefully downhill, through a gap in a stone wall. Coming to a road, turn left. You reach the large **car park** above Líndos near **Supermarket Flora** over to the left (**8; 2h10min**). Now cross the road diagonally left and take the narrow main road downhill to the square in the centre of **Líndos village (9; 2h20min)**, where you'll find your bus stop.

Maria's Taverna

A plethora of tavernas confronts visitors to Líndos, some good, some indifferent. Maria's is worth seeking out: from the main square follow signs to the Acropolis. When you reach the Church of the Panagía, with tower and courtyard on the left, turn right. This street leads through Líndos to St Paul's Bay. At a right/left kink in the street, turn down the street on the left; Maria's is just on the right. Very good air conditioning and an excellent menu compensate for the lack of an outside area.

A short distance further along the street towards St Paul's Bay is **Arxondíko**, an up-market (dinner only) restaurant in an old Lindian mansion, with a roof-top terrace — ideal for special occasions (€€€).

Mythos (€€) is but one of many similar Líndos tavernas, but with quite a good menu and an excellent view over the village towards the sea and the Acropolis. To locate it, leave the main square by the road uphill to the right, alongside the donkey station; Mythos is then on the right. Many Greek specialities, including *kléftiko*, *youvétsi*, *stifádo*, *mousaká* and grills.

MARIA'S TAVERNA
Líndos (2244 031744; mariastavernalindos.com; daily 11.45-23.15 €€

A chance to try Lindian shrimp risotto (same as the small, sweet Sími shrimps), avocado with honey and walnuts, and *bouyoúrdi* (a local name for *saganáki sto foúrno*), plus the special of the day, etc. A good cold CAIR retsína goes especially well with lunch.

restaurants

eat

Garídes piláfi (Shrimp risotto)

Although this photograph shows Maria's small sweet Sími shrimps, shrimp risotto was the dish of the day when we were last there. It's very

tasty and easily made with pre-cooked and peeled shrimps — a great meal in one pot.

There are choices to make. Whole unpeeled fresh prawns add more flavour but can be messy to eat — more fun, but have plenty of napkins to hand. Or use fresh prawns/shrimps and peel before cooking, then strain the liquid and use it to cook the rice. Or buy ready-cooked, to save on the preparation.

Heat the oil in a large pan and cook the onions and garlic until they are translucent. Add the peppers, mushrooms and celery and cook until softened. Add the tomatoes and seasonings and cook gently for about 10 min, then add the rice and *uncooked* prawns/shrimps. (Add ready-cooked just before the rice is done.)

Stir well and simmer for 15 min. Keep an eye on the liquid, adding water as necessary, until it's absorbed and the rice is cooked. If using cooked prawns/shrimps, add to the mixture just before the rice is ready, then the optional crumbled *féta* cheese and/or peas.

<u>Ingredients (for 4 people)</u>

500 g prawns/shrimps, rinsed and cleaned, or 400 g already peeled and cooked
3 tbsp olive oil
1 small onion, chopped
1 garlic clove, crushed
1 large red pepper, chopped
200 g button mushrooms, whole
2 sticks celery, chopped (optional)
400 g tin chopped tomatoes
1/2 tsp oregano
salt & pepper
200-300 g long grain rice
100 g crumbled *féta* cheese (optional)
100 g fresh (cooked) or frozen peas (optional)

Melizanosaláta (Roasted aubergine dip) not illustrated

This dish is a popular *mezé* starter. Wrap a couple of aubergines in foil and bake in the oven at 180° C/gas mark 4 for an hour or more, until *very* soft. (To get the distinctive smoky flavour of an authentic *saláta*, the aubergines must be cooked on a barbecue.) Scoop out the flesh and beat until smooth. Add seasonings to taste: garlic (mashed to a creamy paste), then olive oil, lemon, salt & pepper. The finished mix should be firm and not sloppy.

Kolokithákia tiganitá (Fried courgettes)

Another great *mezé* starter; we're always asking for them, even if they're not on the menu! Really quick and easy to prepare, but they need to be eaten *immediately*.

Top and tail washed courgettes, then slice into thin rings. (If using small or baby courgettes, slice them lengthwise, as in the photograph.) Dust in seasoned flour and fry in about 5 cm of hot oil until browned. Drain on kitchen paper and serve at once.

Courgette flowers (shown above) are also delicious battered and fried — they can be stuffed with *féta*.

Ingredients (for 4 people)
0.5 kg courgettes
seasoned flour
oil for frying

recipes

eat

There are many variations on the **mousakás** theme, but all basically contain the same ingredients. It's a matter of personal taste how you put them together. Some recipes use only aubergines; others (including ours), potato. Anything goes; it depends a great deal on the flavouring.

This is an easy recipe to adjust for any number of people. Even the topping can be a straightforward cheese sauce, béchamel, or one containing egg yolk. We use the béchamel option in this recipe, but it's worth experimenting with the different options.

Frying the aubergines and potatoes can turn this into a very oily (but very tasty) dish. But the aubergine slices can be brushed with oil and baked or dry-fried. Our long-used method is to layer the aubergine (1 cm thick slices) in a dish, drizzling a little oil over each layer: cover with clingfilm and microwave until soft, around 8-10min. Halve the potatoes and boil them until almost cooked.

Mousakás (Moussaka)

Pre-cook the aubergines and potatoes as above. Heat some oil in a frying pan and gently stir-fry the onions and garlic to soften. Add the meat and brown, still stirring. Drain off any excess fat/liquid. Now add the herbs, spices, and salt & pepper to taste. Moisten with the tomato juice if using tinned. Grease a 2.5 l ovenproof dish or large casserole.

Place a layer of aubergine slices in the base of the dish, then the meat. Top with a further layer of aubergine slices and the chopped tomatoes. Finally, place a layer of sliced potatoes on the top.

For the sauce, make a roux with the flour and butter by melting the butter and combining with the flour then, using a balloon whisk, gradually add the milk and seasoning. Continue to stir over the heat until the mixture boils and thickens. (If using a microwave, melt the butter, then add the flour using a balloon whisk to combine the two, and microwave on high for 40 seconds. Gradually whisk in the milk and seasoning. Microwave on high for 2 min, stir, then continue in

1 min bursts, stirring in between, until the sauce bubbles and thickens. Watch carefully, to prevent the mixture boiling over.)

Spread the sauce over the mixture in the dish, sprinkle over some grated cheese and bake at 180° C/gas mark 4 for 30-40 min, until brown on top.

The *mousaká* can be frozen for a few weeks or left overnight on the chiller tray in the fridge, which will enhance the flavour.

Alternative vegetarian version: Replace the meat with about 100 g of cooked puy or green lentils and a mixture of sliced vegetables. For example, heat some olive oil and butter in a frying pan, soften 2 onions, then add 2 sliced carrots, 2 sliced sticks of celery, 4 large chopped tomatoes (or a 400 g tin of tomatoes), a handful of fresh parsley, salt & pepper and an optional dash of red or white wine. Simmer for around 30 min, then add the cooked lentils. Use as the meat layer in the main dish.

Alternative topping: Use the basic sauce recipe above, seasoned with salt & pepper, then stir in 1 egg yolk and 60 g of grated cheese.

Ingredients (for 6 people)
500 g lamb or beef, minced
2-3 pre-cooked aubergines (1 kilo)
2 pre-cooked medium potatoes
2 medium onions, chopped
3 garlic cloves, crushed
1 tin (400 g) plum (or chopped)
  tomatoes, or 4 large ripe
  tomatoes, skinned & chopped
1 tsp basil
1 tsp oregano
1 tsp allspice
salt & pepper to taste
olive or other oil (to drizzle over
  the aubergines and for frying)

For the sauce:
600 ml warmed milk
2 tbsp flour
60 g butter
1/2 tsp nutmeg
2 bay leaves
ground black pepper

Mount Akramítis, the second-highest peak on Rhodes at 823m/2700ft, tops Profítis Ilías (Walk 7) by 21m. We climb to the tiny church of Ág Ioánnes and return the same way, but suggest alternatives. Farm ruins and deserted fields lie en route, now abandoned for easier living elsewhere, and the mountain is left to walkers.

mount akramítis

WALK

The walk begins at the **lay-by** (**1**) on the east side of the Siána–Monólithos road. The path is on the opposite side of the road, marked at time of writing with a bright yellow tarp wrapped around a tree (there is also a red dot). Clamber up the bank and head into the woods. After 70m/yds, turn sharp left on a narrower path, which widens out to a stony, steeply rising trail. After 420m, at a junction marked with a cairn and red dot (**2**), turn right. *(The trail ahead is the return route for an Alternative return.)* The climb is steep, but cypresses provide some shade and viewpoints a good excuse to stop. When the trail makes a zigzag, you will

Distance: 6.6km/4.1mi; 3h

Grade: strenuous, with an ascent/descent of 340m/1115ft; you must be sure-footed and agile. Red dot and cairn waymarks. Sun and shade

Equipment: see page 27; plenty of water

Transport: There is no convenient bus to Monólithos. 🚗 the walk starts at a lay-by on the Monólithos–Siána road, 850m northeast of Monólithos (36° 8.298'N, 27° 44.760'E).

Refreshments: Christós Corner Taverna at the road junction in Monólithos; none en route

Alternatives: use the map and our GPS tracks to (1) carry on to the trig point and ruined firewatch house on the summit (**10**) and return the same way (9km/5.6mi; 4h; +100m/330ft of ascent); (2) climb to the summit, then vary the return as shown on the map, perhaps detouring to a war memorial by Liméri Cave (**11**) (10.2km/6.3mi; 450m/1475ft ascent/descent; 5h)

notice from the retaining walls that it has clearly long been an old route up to the pastures cradled within the mountain range.

The path levels out for a short distance as you enter the **pine tree belt** (**3**; **45min**), allowing you to relax after a steady climb. *Small* red dots are still seen from time to time, as you follow the path atop a retaining wall. At a **junction** (**4**; **1h**), turn right (northeast). *(The trail to the left, southwest, is used for an Alternative return.)* Red-painted arrows indicate the two directions here. This path is narrower, with soft pine needles underfoot, until it starts to descend and is again stony.

A good few minutes later you descend into the bowl of a valley. The path stays mostly to the left side and, after passing a **ruin** (**5**) on the left, rises at the far end of the valley into a smaller abandoned field. Rise again, through a **gap in a wall** (**6**;

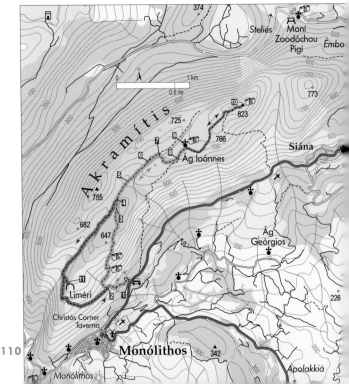

1h15min), into a large flat area. Just 170m from the gap in the wall, *ignore* a smaller path straight on/left. Curve right at this **junction** (**7**), going through another **stone wall** marked with red dots after about 10m. Another rocky ascent follows. The woods thin out, and the sea comes into view.

On the ascent to Ág Ioánnes

At another **junction** (**8**; where a more direct path to the chapel rises from the layby below), continue on a clear path across a meadow. The chapel comes into view. You have to climb over a wooden barrier to keep out goats. Inside the compound (actually a water cistern) you come to **Ág Ioánnes** (**9**; **1h40min**). This tiny 800-year-old church has long been a shelter and water source for the local goatherds and farmers. Set high amidst a rocky wilderness, it's a peaceful place just to soak in the atmosphere and admire the views.

Return the same way to the **lay-by on the Siána road** (**3h**) … unless you are doing one of the Alternative walks on page 109.

Christós Corner Taverna

A taverna commanding an excellent elevated location, at the road junction in Monólithos, Christós Corner offers a delicious choice of Greek cuisine. Our readers love it! There is a huge selection of *mezédes* to sample before you even make a start on the specialities and grills. You could be there for hours — everything is so tasty, including the house wine. Their *gígantes* are among the best we've ever tasted. Ingredients are fresh and mostly local produce. Easy to make, *tirokeftédes* are always tucked into with relish. See recipe and photo opposite, ingredients below:

CHRISTÓS CORNER TAVERNA
Monólithos (2246 061310; **daily in season from 08.00 to 22.00** €€

very wide menu; some **highlights** include:

bakaliáraki tiganitó (fried cod balls)

tirokeftédes (cheese balls)

melitzanosaláta (aubergine dip)

omelettes, salads, *mousakás*

charcoal grilled specialities: lamb, goat and special village sausage

house **dry white wine** excellent, with a hint of muscat

Tirokeftédes: ingredients (for 20 cheese balls)

300 g grated hard cheese (gouda, *kasseri, regato*, etc, or cheddar)

60 g SR flour (or plain with 1/2 tsp baking powder)

2 eggs

restaurants

eat

Gígantes (Giant butter beans in sauce)

Soak the beans in plenty of water overnight. Strain, then cover with water again and boil gently for about 40 min. Don't overcook the beans; they need to be *just* cooked without being too soft.

Mix together all the other ingredients, stir in the beans, then place in a greased tin or dish and cover with foil. Bake at 200° C/gas mark 6 for 30-40 min. Check towards the end of the cooking time, and add extra water/ tomato juice and/or seasoning if necessary. Serve hot or cold — as a starter or as a vegetable.

Tirokeftédes (Cheese balls)

Beat the eggs and combine with the other ingredients *(listed opposite)*. Roll pieces of the mixture into small walnut-sized balls. Dust lightly with flour and fry in very hot oil, enough to cover, for a just few minutes.

Ingredients (for 6 people, as a
  starter)
250 g dried butter beans (or 3
  x 400 g tins)
2 garlic cloves, crushed
100 ml olive oil
3 large ripe tomatoes, skinned &
  chopped (or 1 x 400 g tin of
  chopped tomatoes)
1 small onion, chopped
1 tsp dried parsley or 1 heaped
  tbsp of fresh flat-leaved
  parsley, shredded
2 level tsp cumin
salt & pepper to taste
Optional: chopped carrot and
  celery can be added to the mix,
  and curry powder instead of
  cumin also works quite well

recipes

eat

This compact walk is full of interesting features. We start at Kritinía Castle, with fine views. Our descent through a gorge is spectacular — and easy into the bargain. An ancient temple awaits by the shore; neglected and forlorn, it feels like a personal discovery. The return to the castle is amazingly direct, straight up the hillside.

kritinía castle

WALK

Kritinía Castle was originally built by the Knights of St John on three levels; each level was assigned to a different Grand Master. Apart from remnants of the chapel, there is little to see inside. **The walk begins** at the main **car park** (**1**): walk downhill past the café/shop to the T-junction at the bend in the access road to the castle and turn right (south). After 160m/yds, where the tarmac ends (at time of writing), turn left at a **junction** (**2**). (The return route enters from the right here.) Ignore two tracks forking left but, some 400m from the junction , as the main track makes a U-bend to the left, go right down a **footpath** (**3**) — just 15m past a rough track off right. After about 200m the path becomes very overgrown, but this doesn't last long, and after 80m it widens out. Follow the path round the contour of the hill.

Distance: 3.1km/1.9mi; 1h25min

Grade: moderate, on tracks and paths (with a very slight possibility of vertigo in a part of the gorge section). The altitude gain from sea level back to the castle is 120m/395ft. Prickly shrubs are invasive in places, so wear long trousers and long sleeves.

Transport: 🚗 car to Kritinía Castle and back. Park anywhere nearby; the walk starts at the main car park (36° 15.819'N, 27° 48.583'E). Be aware that there may be two ladies, one on the road up to the castle, the other opposite the castle, who accost the unwary traveller during the tourist season. They claim responsibility for keeping the castle clean and tidy and say they do not get paid. The second lady may demand €1 for parking up at the castle. They're both neat little income-generators, and there's no reason to feel you have to comply!

Refreshments: There is a wide choice of tavernas in Kámiros Skála and Kritinía. The elevated platia in Kritinía is a pleasant place to linger and enjoy the view over the country-side; Taverna Piatsa here serves Greek specialities. There is a café at the nearby Mylos folklore museum and a café/shop just below Kritinía Castle, but nothing en route.

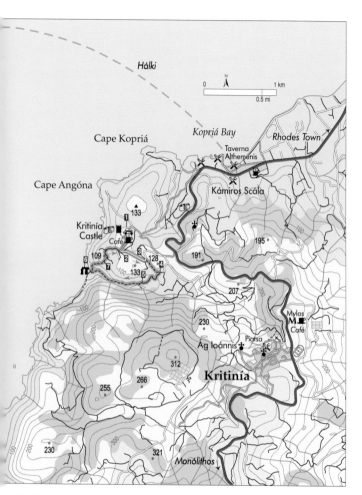

Under 50m further on (300m from **3**), you meet a rough track at a **T-junction** (**4**). Greenhouses are not far ahead. Turn right downhill here, descending steadily towards the **gorge**. At the end of an orchard on the left, you may spot the first red way-marking dots! Ignore a track going sharp left and continue on the main track. As this track ends, keep ahead along the top edge of a field on the left for half a minute, then continue ahead as indicated by a **red arrow** (**5**; **25min**). Ignore a downhill path almost at once, and stay alongside a **wall** on the right. The path edges the side of the gorge on the left and may be slightly vertiginous in places. Views open up to the sea ahead through the V of the gorge. As the path descends to the bottom of the valley (**45min**), stay on the path to the right, with a **wire fence** to your left. You reach the shore at an **ancient temple** (**6**; **50min**); partly excavated, it has been abandoned to the elements.

To return, go right around the end of the fence (taking care at the edge of the cliff), and follow the path uphill (blue dot, red arrow). The well-defined path initially parallels the coast more or less, but after several minutes it heads more inland. Ascend through a rock channel (**7**; **1h05min**), to a **wire fence.** Keep the fence on your right (blue and red dots); behind it is an olive grove, on the far side of which are three white houses. When you reach the access road for these three houses, turn left. Now just navigate towards the castle, in view ahead. Ignore three tracks off left (the first an access track to an overgrown tennis court, the second to a field, the third just where the main track is concreted for a few metres). This main track takes you back to **2**, from where you retrace steps to **Kritinía Castle** (**1h25min**).

Kámiros Skála from Althemenis Fish Restaurant

Kámiros Skála is usually a peaceful backwater. Most of the activity revolves around the arrival of the ferry from Hálki and local fishing boats. It can be quite interesting when a boat load of sheep arrives and they have to be transferred onto the quay! For the most part though, the only sound is the gentle whooshing of waves on the shingle and muted conversation.

restaurants
eat

Althemenis Fish Restaurant

Three tavernas beckon at Kámiros Skála. **Loukas** is opposite the entrance to the harbour. If this doesn't appeal, turn into the harbour road and park in the car park on the left. There is a pleasant taverna in a corner past this car park, **Amythita**.

> **ALTHEMENIS FISH RESTAURANT**
> Kámiros Skála
> open daily in season €€
> English menu available
>
> large selection of **mezés**, and Sími shrimps feature — as well as yummy *tirokeftédes* (cheese balls)
>
> the **speciality is fish**, and *skordaliá* (garlic dip) is an essential accompaniment to fish here, even with *kolokithákia* (fried courgette)
>
> limited choice of **meat** dishes

But we prefer **Althemenis Fish Restaurant**, to the right (with parking). We think it has the *best* position, by the water. The prices, in kilos for fish, are quite good, and the menu as a whole extensive. (See page 12 about ordering fish by weight.) The seal of approval regarding its popularity is the number of Greek clients, especially at weekends and holidays.

If on the other hand you are driving to Rhodes Town from Kritinía and are looking for a place en route, try **Taverna Akrogiáli** at the Kritinía end of Kalavárda. We often stop off here, to enjoy the ambience. Choose from traditional Greek fare and fish. It's a typical Greek fish taverna on the edge of the shore, with a cameo view overlooking a small sandy beach with fishing boats and tamarisk trees. Along the same road, note **Deipnos Cook & Grill**, across the road from the airport. We haven't eaten there yet, and comments on Trip Advisor are not inspiring, but it could be a good fall-back for those whose flights are held up for an hour or two — an excellent escape from the confines of a hot (and probably overcrowded) airport.

Marídes tiganités (Fried whitebait)

Fish like *marídes* and *atherina* are eaten whole and go well with oúzo. These are easy to cope with if self-catering. When buying, the smaller the fish the better. This method also works well at home with whitebait. Allow about 200 g of small fish per person. If serving as a *mezé*, the

quantity will depend on how many other dishes are offered.

Wash and dry the fish and coat with seasoned flour, shaking off excess flour. Heat some light oil (*not* olive oil) in a deep pan (fill to a depth of at least 5 cm), until very hot. Fry the fish in the hot oil until brown — which won't take long. Drain on kitchen paper and serve with lemon quarters.

Skordaliá (Garlic dip) *not illustrated*

A very popular sauce on Rhodes — and easy to make. Traditionally served with fish, it also goes well with beetroot and *hórta* (see page 14).

Boil the potatoes in their skins. When cool, discard the skins and mash well. Add the garlic paste a little at a time, until you achieve the strength you want.

Ingredients (for 4 people)
450 g large floury potatoes
8 garlic cloves, mashed into a
   creamy paste
50 ml olive oil
25 ml white wine vinegar
salt & pepper

Gradually blend in the olive oil, vinegar and salt & pepper, until the mixture is creamy (but not sloppy) and to the required taste.

recipes

eat

Horiátiki saláta (Greek salad)

Traditionally made *without* lettuce, this salad comes in many variations. It can be served with sliced lettuce or sliced white cabbage (usually when fresh lettuce isn't easily available). The lettuce or cabbage is placed in the base of the serving dish and the other ingredients layered on the top. Alternatively, the ingredients are tossed together with cubed *féta* cheese. Anything goes!

Greek salad at Christós Corner (Walk 9), with shredded white cabbage below the *féta*, and pickled chillis adding a final touch

Place the ingredients in a serving dish as shown here, with slabs of *féta* cheese on top. Olive oil is drizzled on the *féta*, along with a sprinkling of dried oregano.

Angourodomáto saláta (Tomato & cucumber salad)

This simple salad is very tasty when you want something light. The tomatoes and cucumber are sliced and drizzled with olive oil, then sprinkled with oregano and salt. Thinly sliced onion can also be included.

Ingredients (for 4 people)

1 fresh lettuce, washed and shredded
3 tomatoes, cut into wedges
1/2 cucumber, sliced or cubed
1 onion, finely sliced
1 green pepper, finely sliced
black olives to taste
250 g *féta* cheese, in thick slices
olive oil & vinegar or lemon
dried oregano & dill (but fresh dill makes this salad really tasty)
salt & pepper

One of the most beautiful places in the Mediterranean, you just cannot go to Rhodes without visiting Líndos. Almost everybody does so by joining an organised coach tour. Do take our advice and plan your own tour, to escape the crowds. Perhaps combine it with the short walk described on page 127.

líndos

EXCURSION

Dozens of coaches arrive at Líndos during the morning, pouring out visitors by the hundreds. All of them tread the same path up through the narrow streets, then swarm over the acropolis. The normal itinerary then is back to the coach and leave — or lunch, then leave.

So devise your own tour! Visitor numbers to the acropolis tend to reduce markedly by 3pm, so the best plan is to have lunch before climbing up to explore it. There is plenty to fill the morning. Curving around the bay and overlooked by the acropolis is a large beach of fine golden sand with plenty of facilities. If you prefer a little more solitude, try the engaging short walk out to the tomb of

Description: allow a full day, to take in the sights, have lunch, and do the short walk described on page 127

Transport: 🚌 or 🚗 to Líndos (as Walk 8, page 99). Parking is not a problem if you drive along the beachside road looking for a metered space or keep going, because there is field parking further on, up the left fork on the sweeping bend (see map on page 100). The further you go, the easier it is to find parking, and it's particularly handy for the beach.

Refreshments: cafés, fast-food outlets, tavernas and restaurants abound in Líndos; see Walk 8.

Overview of Excursions 1 and 2

Kleoboulos described on page 127. It's on the northern tip of the bay and will give you a wholly different perspective on Líndos.

Tourist shops, coffee bars, and fast-food outlets pack the narrow, winding, climbing streets of the village. Little churches are tucked away in these streets, too, and some fine old traditional houses built by wealthy ship-owners in the 17th to 19th centuries. Except for a high ornate wall and a heavily decorated door there is little to see but, occasionally, a door is left ajar. A glimpse through the doorway reveals a flower-filled courtyard with a floor of decorative pebbles. Black and white pebbles are favoured and used rather like a Roman mosaic to make a design or motif. This style of pebble floors, known as *hocklákí*, is popular on Rhodes and widely used. Unfortunately, these traditional *arxondíko* houses are diminishing, many being converted into restaurants and shops.

If you wander the streets, keeping inland of the acropolis hill, you can easily reach St Paul's Bay on the south side of the town. Just keep the acropolis to the left as you meander through the narrow streets and, when you get a more open view, you can see the remains of an ancient theatre below the acropolis.

The small, almost land-locked bay of St Paul's does have a small beach, and development is taking place there slowly but steadily (there is also plenty of car parking space). St Paul visited Rhodes on his way from Miletus to Syria to help convert the island to Christianity, and it's believed he landed here. The small church tucked away on the far side of the bay is dedicated to him.

If you don't want to struggle up the hill to the acropolis, you can take the romantic option and travel by donkey to the castle, pretending you are a knight on horseback. By the afternoon many of the lace-sellers lining the route have lost their appetite for pressing tourists to buy their beautiful work. Some of it is made by hand by the local ladies over the winter months, but imports have added volume and variety.

When you have finally climbed 116m/380ft, almost to the top of this flat-topped outcrop of rock, you reach the pay booth. Too late now to change your mind!

Location is everything, and this huge rock defends two natural harbours which has made it a desirable residence ever since man first formed settlements. Occupation can be traced back to the Neolithic Age (2500-2000 BC), but it was not until around the 10th century BC that Líndos really rose to prominence — along with two other cities of antiquity on the island, Kámiros and Ialyssós. A temple dedicated to Athena Líndos has existed on this rock from at least that period.

Kleoboulos, who governed the city for 40 years in the 6th century BC, ruled moderately and wisely and drew great respect from all over Greece. He was one of the 'Seven Sages' of Ancient Greece. By this time Líndos had become a great maritime trading city and had extended its trade zone to include Egypt, Cyprus and Syria. With the growing stature of the city, Kleoboulos improved the sanctuary to Athena by building a larger temple, thought to have had a four-columned portico at each end but without columns along the sides. The archaic staircase seen below the modern one may also be his contribution.

Around 342 BC the temple built by Kleoboulos burnt down, together with the statue of Athena and many of the votive offerings. The Lindians promptly built a new one in its place, repeating the original style, but with an even bigger statue showing Athena standing and not seated as in the original. The statue this time was built with a body of gold-plated wood and limbs of marble.

Later, in the Hellenistic Period around 200 BC, further developments took place on the acropolis, which brought it to its final form. A huge double-winged covered colonnade, a *stoa,* was added on the north side, embracing the steps up to the propylaeum and covering the whole width of the entrance. A small temple built in the northwest corner is thought to be Roman. On the western outer flank of the acropolis is a 4th-century BC theatre cut into the rock, with 27 rows of seats still preserved. If you did not see this walking over to St Paul's Bay, you can get a good view looking over the walls. Also outside the acropolis and near the theatre are the foundations of ancient walls believed to have formed part of a gymnasium.

View from the acropolis across Lindos Bay towards the Kleoboulos Tomb (behind the left-hand column)

The present fortifications are the work of the Knights of St John who, in the Byzantine era, remodelled and strengthened the walls of an earlier fortification. Restoration is a permanent feature these days — so expect scaffolding.

Tomb of Kleoboulos

See map on page 100

Distance: 4.4km/2.7mi; 1h35min

Grade: easy, waymarked path, with a short climb to the tomb

Equipment: see page 27

Transport, Refreshments: as Walk 8, page 98

Start the walk from the **main square in Líndos** (**9**): walk uphill, as if leaving the village, then turn right after 20m/yds on the road to the beach. As this bends right five minutes later, ascend the lane on the left signposted 'Kleoboulos Tomb'. Just before this lane becomes a gravel car park, go along the walled-in path to the left of the gateway. The path soon leaves the walls behind and emerges in a very stony landscape. In around 10 minutes, you come to a **memorial** (**10**) to a long-serving local politician who hailed from Líndos.

Windmill en route to the Tomb of Kleoboulos; take care if you go inside!

Over to the right is Líndos, and ahead is the rotunda (tomb), at the end of the promontory. The path skirts to the left of a deep inlet, then heads through a gap in the wall to the **windmill** shown above (**11**;**35min**). Beware of the dangerous state of the interior if venturing inside. Pick up the path again behind the windmill and skirt another smaller inlet. Cairns guide the way through the rocks as the path ascends a rocky outcrop to the **Tomb of Kleoboulos** (**12**; **50min**); see history on pages 125-126.

Return the same way.

There is a huge choice of sailings from Rhodes to different islands. We have chosen Kastellórizo, the most easterly island in Greece. Although it lies a fair distance away (72 nautical miles and very close to Kaş in Turkey), the journey by fast catamaran only takes about 2h30min, leaving five hours to explore.

kastellórizo

EXCURSION

Kastellórizo is the modern name for the island, which was called Megísti in ancient times. Legend tells that Megisthus, a Cretan prince, was the first settler and named the island after himself. Perhaps less romantic is the suggestion that the name arose because it's largest of all the fourteen small islands spread around the area. The present name came into use during the Crusades as a

Description: a full day out, with 5h on board the catamaran and 5h to explore Kastellórizo; *see overview map on page 123*

Transport: ⚓ from Rhodes Town (departs from 19 on the plan inside the front cover). Cost about €40 when booked well in advance. It's windy on deck travelling at speed, but there is plenty of inside cabin space for both smokers and non-smokers, and the journey is smooth enough usually to settle into a good book.

Refreshments: ample cafés, tavernas and restaurants

corruption of 'Kastel Roso', the name of the castle built from the island's red rocks. Five hours ashore is perfect for this picturesque tiny island, just 9 sq km (3.5 sq mi), with less than 300 hundred inhabitants. It leaves enough time to explore the main town by taking the short walk outlined on the following pages and then enjoy a good lunch.

Like many Greek islands, Kastellórizo has had a chequered history. There are footsteps of the Minoans and Myceneans from early times and, later, the Romans, Lycians, Greeks, Egyptians, Turks, Venetians, French and Italians. Now it's administered from Rhodes.

The island came under Turkish rule in 1537 and, granted special trading privileges, it flourished for a time. During the 19th century the population had increased to 9000 inhabitants, supported by a good trade from sponge fishing. It was in this period of wealth that many of its churches and fine houses were built.

Kastellórizo entered a period of turbulence as it tried to break free from the Turks. In its final attempt, the uprising was put down by France (as an ally of Italy); France then used the island as a base for operations against Syria. In the First World War Kastellórizo was bombarded from the Turkish coast. Italy took control in 1921, restricted trade, and tried to de-Hellenise the island. Damage caused by the earthquake of 1927 was not repaired by the Italians, and the island's prosperity declined further, with many starting to emigrate. By 1940 the population was estimated to be around 1400. When the Italians surrendered in 1943, freedom appeared to be in sight when the British arrived, but the island continued to suffer severe bombing raids from the Germans. Eventually, in 1947, it was reunited with Greece — but not before yet more of the populace had left for a life elsewhere.

There are many stories to tell of the thousands who left Kastellórizo, principally for Australia, to find work and start again. Lots of these 'Kassies', as they call themselves, are still proud of their island and have returned to reclaim and renovate their old homes, but few remain as permanent residents.

A first surprise on entering the harbour is the rather striking Turkish mosque and minaret on the headland, but your first impression may be just how serene this rocky island looks. Colourful houses interspersed with shops and tavernas ribbon the deep, natural harbour — all guarded by the remains of a

Crusader castle on the hill above the mosque. This port town, **Megísti**, is the largest on the island and is split into two parts, Pigádia around the port, and Horáfia over the hill beyond the castle. The walk described below takes a look at both parts. If you just prefer

Distance: 5km/3mi; allow 2h
Grade: easy, although there are plenty of steps (ascending about 100m/300ft overall)
Equipment: good walking shoes, ample water
Refreshments: only at the start and finish

to relax, stop at the Megísti Hotel, where there is an attractive terrace with sun beds for hire. The water in the harbour sparkles with clarity and is good for swimming or snorkelling.

Our walking tour never strays too far from the port where the boat awaits your return so, if you feel time is running away, there is always a direct route back. Although this ranks little more than a stroll, it's packed with interest, including the mosque, museum, castle, windmill and Lycian tomb.

Turn right on leaving the boat, and walk all the way around the **harbour square** to the **Megísti Hotel** at the furthest point. On the way you pass a church with a clock tower, **St George of the Well**. Turn around at the hotel and walk back the same way, to get a different view of the harbour and to start the walk below.

Walking tour of Megísti

Start the walk at **St George of the Well**: turn right here, to walk down its left side; go left, then right, to find the church of **St Mercurius**. Return to the harbourside to continue, and notice

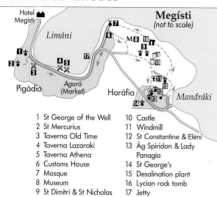

Hotel Megísti

Limáni

Megísti
(not to scale)

Pigádia

Agorá
(Market)

Horáfia

Mandráki

1 St George of the Well
2 St Mercurius
3 Taverna Old Time
4 Taverna Lazaraki
5 Taverna Athena
6 Customs House
7 Mosque
8 Museum
9 St Dimitri & St Nicholas
10 Castle
11 Windmill
12 St Constantine & Eléni
13 Ág Spiridon & Lady
   Panagía
14 St George's
15 Desalination plant
16 Lycian rock tomb
17 Jetty

the old *agorá*, the **market** building. Walking
the final straight side
of the harbour, it's
easy to pick out the
mosque, castle and
windmill which line
the ongoing route.

Nearing the end of
the harbour, go right
alongside the

Customs House, with the **mosque** now on your left. Climb the
steps to arrive at the **museum** (07.00-14.00; cl Mon) and walk
along the front of it, with the museum on your left. The route
now heads above and parallel with the port *(limáni)*, so there are
good views down over it. At a T-junction of more major steps,
turn left uphill, quickly reaching the twin churches of **Ág
Nikólaos** and **Ág Dimítri** on the left. Just beyond are the
remains of a **castle** restored by the Knights of St John in 1309.
Steps take you up the remains and a vertical iron ladder
completes the ascent. From the top you can appreciate the twin
nature of the churches when you see the two adjacent barrel-
vaulted roofs and enjoy a view of the scattered islands and the
Turkish mainland.

A paved path complete with lamp posts leads from the castle
towards Horáfia, passing the old **windmill** on the way. A few
minutes later you reach a road and enter a huge square with a
school and churches. This is Horáfia. The important church to

see here is **St Constantine and Eléni**, on the left (within the school complex), built in 1835 of granite from the temple of Apollo brought from Patara in Turkey. Possibly only Sunday and Holy Day visitors will find it open. Still on the left there are two churches together, **Our Lady Panagía** and, set back a little, the smaller **Ág Spirídon**. The huge twin-towered church opposite, on the far side of the square, is **St George's**, built in 1903 on the remains of an earlier church. In the middle is a monument to Despiná Achladiotou, a remarkable lady who lived to a ripe old age. She is remembered for her defiance in resisting evacuation during World War II, raising the Greek flag each day and co-operating with the allies.

Turn left out of the square to follow the road downhill towards the seafront, passing the schoolyard on the left. At the bottom, first turn left behind the houses, then continue almost immediately to the coast and up the gravel drive leading towards a house. Before reaching the house, take the footpath which continues to follow the shore for a short while, before turning down paved steps and meeting steps downhill opposite (coming from between the castle and windmill). There is a small church on the left here, as well as the island's desalination plant.

Turn right and follow the paved walkway around the coast back towards the harbour. If you can take your eyes away from the seascape with the offshore islands, watch out for the sign on the left to the **Lycian tomb**. There are yet more steps to climb, but the tomb is a fine, undamaged example and worth seeing. Return to the path and follow it to the **mosque** on the headland, passed on the outward route. The **harbour** is now just ahead.

Taverna Old Story – Old Time

The taverna where we had lunch when researching this excursion a few years ago is no more, surprisingly. But the strangely named taverna Old Story – Old Time is in the same location, at the waterside, and similarly shaded by vines. It's a pleasant retreat from the main activity and bustle of the harbour, and you can often have lunch while watching a loggerhead sea turtle (*Caretta caretta*) nearby! The food is good and freshly prepared. Old Time has a fairly traditional menu (€€), with a mix of meat and fish dishes. Their stuffed onions are especially tasty, and try the zucchini and chickpea fritters.

For those wanting to be closer to quayside activity, **Tavernas Athena** and **Lazaráki** sit side by side further along the harbour, in the centre.

restaurants

eat

Spanakópita (Spinach pie)

Wash the spinach well, dry it, trim off thick stems, and shred. Heat the oil in a frying pan and cook the onion, garlic, spring onions (and leek, if used) until soft. Add the herbs, then the spinach, and toss the mixture until the spinach wilts and excess moisture evaporates.

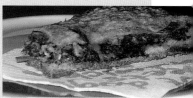

Stir in the féta and add pepper and salt to taste. Remember, the cheese will be fairly salty. (Lancashire creamy or crumbly cheese — even mixed with grated cheddar — make good substitutes for *féta*.)

Prepare a 26 cm x 20 cm oblong dish or tin (like a large lasagne dish) or 20 cm round dish or tin and lightly oil. Roll out your pastry of choice, or butter and layer about 5 sheets of filo pastry, and line the dish or tin.

Fill with the spinach and cheese mixture, then cover with another layer of pastry or filo, sealing the edges. Make slits in the top to allow steam to escape, and brush with egg or milk. Sesame seeds can be also scattered over the crust before baking.

Bake at 180° C/gas mark 4 for around 30 min, until the pastry is golden brown. Serve hot or cold.

Ingredients (for 4 people)
- 500 g fresh spinach
- 150 g onions and/or spring onions, chopped
- 1 large leek, washed and chopped (optional)
- 2 garlic cloves, crushed
- 200 g *féta* cheese
- 1.5 tsp dried dill or 2 tbsp fresh, chopped
- 1.5 tsp dried parsley or 2 tbsp fresh, flat-leaved, chopped
- 75 ml olive oil
- salt & pepper

For the pastry
- 400 g filo *or* 450 g puff *or* 425 g shortcrust

recipes

eat

Yemistá me kimá (Stuffed peppers and tomatoes)

Peppers, large tomatoes, large courgettes and aubergines can all be stuffed with the rice and meat or rice stuffing. A very popular lunchtime dish — but very filling. For this recipe allow one stuffed vegetable per person as a starter, two or three for a main meal. For a vegetarian version, omit the mince (kimá) and double the rice.

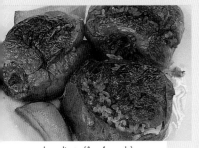

Cut off the tops of the peppers and tomatoes and set aside. Hollow out the insides. Chop and save the tomato pulp. (If preferred, the whole peppers can be blanched in boiling water for around 3 min, then drained well and cooled before filling.)

Brown the mince and soften the onion in some of the olive oil, add the tomato pulp, garlic (if used), rice, half the parsley, and salt & pepper. Simmer for around 8 min, until the liquid is absorbed. Check that the rice doesn't stick, and add extra tomato juice or stock if needed. Add the pine nuts and raisins (if used). Mix well together, spoon into the hollow tomatoes and peppers and replace the tops.

Ingredients (for 4 people)
6 tomatoes
4 red peppers
500 g lean minced meat
125 g short grain rice
1 onion
2 garlic cloves, crushed (optional)
500 ml passata or 1 x 400 g
  tin chopped tomatoes (sieved)
100 ml olive oil
3 tbsp fresh parsley, chopped
50 g pine nuts (optional)
50 g raisins (optional)
1/2 tsp cumin (optional)
salt & pepper
breadcrumbs (optional)

Note: Cooked left-over rice can be used in *yemistá*. After browning the mince, etc, add the other ingredients and cooked rice. Simmer until the excess moisture is driven off, then use to stuff the vegetables.

Pack the stuffed vegetables firmly in a greased dish or roasting tin. Pour over the remaining olive oil and tomato juice. Sprinkle over the breadcrumbs (if used). Cover the dish tightly with foil and bake for about 45 min at 180° C/gas mark 4. Remove the foil and bake a further 10 min.

Variations: The same filling can be used to make *papoutsákia* (stuffed aubergines and courgettes; literally 'little shoes'). Cut the courgettes lengthwise or aubergines in half. Scoop out the pulp and save to cook with the filling. Brush some lemon juice in the empty cases to prevent them discolouring. A large tin of chopped tomatoes replaces the tomatoes in the main recipe. Top with béchamel sauce (made with 1 heaped tbsp of flour, 25 g butter, 200 ml milk, 1 small egg and a pinch of ground nutmeg). After filling the vegetable cases with the cooked mixture, spoon over the sauce and sprinkle with grated cheese. Place in a shallow tray or dish and bake, uncovered, at 180° C/gas mark 4 for 30-40 min.

Tzatzíki (Yoghurt dip) *not illustrated*

The ubiquitous accompaniment to most Greek meals. There is often a raised eyebrow if this isn't part of your order but, of course, it's not to everyone's taste.

Squeeze as much liquid out of the cucumber as possible and mix well with the yoghurt. Add the garlic to taste (you may not want it too strong), a touch of olive oil, a little salt & pepper, and dill if used. Garnish with olives to serve. Taste as you go!

Ingredients (for 4 people)
250 g strained yoghurt (see shopping tips, page 31)
1 small cucumber, coarsely grated
2-3 garlic cloves, crushed (or sometimes finely grated)
olive oil
salt & pepper
fresh dill, chopped (optional)
fresh olives (garnish)

Not many people visiting Greece on a casual basis find the **Greek language** easy to get to grips with. The first obstacle is the Greek alphabet itself. It uses a fair number of characters not represented in the Latin alphabet. In many situations, particularly with place names, road signs and even menus, it is deemed important to change the Greek over to the Latin alphabet to make the names more understandable to foreigners. Unfortunately, there is no definitive or official way to change Greek letters to their Latin equivalent for some of the reasons outlined below. This itself just adds to the confusion, as you will see.

Learning one or two of the pitfalls shown here should help with reading menus in tavernas and with some pronunciations.

The trouble with 'g': On the face of it, this seems a fairly straightforward transliteration. The problem is that 'g' is pronounced as 'y' when preceding 'i' or 'e', but as 'g' in other instances. So a word like *gemistá* (meaning 'stuffed', as in tomatoes or peppers}, is often written as *yemistá* — the way it is pronounced. *Ágios,* meaning 'saint', is another common word regularly mispronounced by visitors. Again the 'g' has a 'y' sound, so it sounds like *áyios.*

The trouble with 'mp': Since the letter 'b' is pronounced as a 'v', it leaves the alphabet without a 'b' sound. To overcome this, a combination of letters, 'mp' is used. This combination is pronounced as 'b' at the start of a word, but as 'mb' anywhere else in the word. The Greek word *mpampou* is a classic illustration. That is how it might be written as a conversion from the Greek alphabet — or equally, it could be written *bambou*. From here it is only a small step to recognise it as 'bamboo'. The mp/mb confusion is commonly noticed on the menu with

GREEK

lamb chops, often seen as 'lamp' chops — which raises a smile with visitors (… but the Greeks would pronounce it as 'lamb' anyway).

'Lamp' cutlets

The trouble with 'nt': This is another combination of letters which is pronounced as a normal 'd' at the beginning of a word and 'nd' elsewhere. It crops up in words like *ntomátes* (tomatoes), which can also appear as *domátes*. This combination is used when a hard 'd' is required, because the 'd' in the Greek alphabet is pronounced as a soft 'd', almost like a 'th'. The word for two, *deo*, for example, is pronounced *theo*.

There are one or two other letter combinations with special pronunciations, but those above are the ones most commonly encountered and the most useful ones to learn.

For place names, menu items and shopping, we have used the transliteration that points the way towards the correct pronunciation, but remember that the stress (´) is important too!

CONVERSION TABLES

Weights		Volume		Oven temperatures		
						gas
10 g	1/2 oz	15 ml	1 tbsp	°C	°F	mark
25 g	1 oz	55 ml	2 fl oz	140°C	275°F	1
50 g	2 oz	75 ml	3 fl oz	150°C	300°F	2
110 g	4 oz	150 ml	1/4 pt	170°C	325°F	3
200 g	7 oz	275 ml	1/2 pt	180°C	350°F	4
350 g	12 oz	570 ml	1 pt	190°C	375°F	5
450 g	1 lb	1 l	1-3/4 pt	200°C	400°F	6
700 g	1 lb 8 oz	1.5 l	2-1/2 pt	220°C	425°F	7
900 g	2 lb			230°C	430°F	8
1.35 g	3 lb			240°C	475°F	9

MENU ITEMS

aláti salt
angoúri cucumber
arakás peas
arní lamb
  kokkinistó in tomoto sauce
  kléftiko in filo parcel with veg/ cheese
  lemonáto in herb sauce with lemon
  brizóles chops
  psitó roast
áspro white
áspro krasí white wine
astakós lobster
atherina small, whitebait-like fish
axionó sea urchin
bakaliáros cod
baklavá filo pastry, nuts soaked in syrup
bámies okra, ladies fingers
barboúni fish similar to red mullet
biftékia mince done as a beefburger
bira beer
bouzákia grilled lamb or goat
briám similar to ratatouille

brizóla chop
deípno dinner
dolmádes vine leaves, rolled and stuffed with mince and rice
domátes tomatoes
  yemistés stuffed with rice, herbs and maybe mince
elaiólado olive oil
eliés olives
Ellinikós kafés Greek coffee (never with milk)
  glykós sweet
  métrios medium sweet
  skétos plain, simple (no sugar)
fasolákia green beans
fáva yellow pea purée
féta feta cheese
  saganáki sto foúrno oven-baked feta with tomatoes and peppers
filéto filet
fráoules strawberries
fréska froúta fresh fruit
galaktoboúreko filo/ custard sweet

galopoúla turkey
galéos cod
  me skordaliá with garlic dip
garídes prawns (pronounced garithes)
g(y)emistá stuffed
g(y)iaoúrti yoghurt
  me méli with honey
g(y)ígantes giant butter beans in sauce
giouvétsi veal in a clay pot with *manéstra*
glyka dessert ('sweet')
g(y)úros meat from large skewer
haloúmi cheese
halvás sesame/ sugar sweet
hoirinó pork
hoiriní brizóla pork chop
horiátiki saláta Greek salad
hortofágos vegetarian
hoúmous hummus
imám baíldi stuffed aubergine
kafés coffee
  frappé iced

me gála with milk
kakáo hot chocolate
kakaviá fish soup
kalamári squid
karídes walnuts
karpoúzi watermelon
kataïfi pastry, like shredded wheat strands, soaked in syrup
katálogos menu
  krasión wine list
katsíki goat
kávouras boiled crab
kimá mince
keftédes fried meatballs
kléftiko see *arní kléftiko*
kolokithákia courgettes
  tiganitá fried
kolokithokeftédes fried courgette balls
kokkinistó veal in tomato sauce
kokteil cocktail
kondosoúvli spiced port on a spit
koniák cognac
kotolétes cutlets

kotópoulo chicken
koukiá broad beans
kounéli rabbit
krasí wine
  áspro or *lefkó* white
  kókkino red
  rozé rosé
krokétes croquettes
kserotígana (thiples) deep-friend pastry
ksifías swordfish
ksúdi vinegar (pronounced kseethi)
ládi oil
lákano cabbage
loukániko sausage
loukoumádes honey-soaked batter balls
makarónia spaghetti
  me kimá bolognaise ('with mince')
manéstra rice-like pasta
manitária mushrooms
marídes small fish (like whitebait)
maroúli lettuce
melekoúni see *pastéli*
méli honey
melitzána aubergine
melitzánosaláta aubergine dip
mesimerianó lunch
mezédes starters (mezés for short)

míla apples
moskári beef or veal
mousakás moussaka
múdia mussels
neró water
nes instant coffee
oktapódi octopus
omeléta omelette
orektiká first course, starters
oúzo aniseed spirit
pagákia ice (cubes)
pagotó ice cream
païdákia lamb chops
papoutsákia half aubergines stuffed with mince, tomato & onions, with a cheese topping
pásta cake, pastry
pastéli sesame and honey bars
pastítsio baked meat and pasta dish
patátes potatoes (often synonymous with chips in tavernas)
  tiganités chips (full description)
patzária beetroot cooked with its leaves
pepóni melon
pipéri pepper
piperiés peppers
  yemistés stuffed

with rice and meat
pita pita bread
pitaroúdia Rhodian-style chickpea patties
pítsa pizza
portokáli oranges
proinó breakfast
psári fish
psarotavérna fish taverna
psetó roast
psomí bread
retsína resinated wine
revíthia chickpeas
revithokeftédes fried chickpea balls
rígani oregano
rúzi rice (pronounced reezee)
rúzogalo rice pudding
saganáki fried cheese starter
saláta salad
saligária snails
  yiáxni in a casserole with tomato sauce
sándouitz sandwich
sardéles sardines
seftaliá home-made sausage
sikóti liver
sikotariá fried liver and kidney
simiakó small sweet shrimps from Sími
skordaliá garlic/

mashed potato dip
skórdo garlic
soúpa soup
soutzoukákia spicy meat rolls
souvláki meat on skewer
spanakópita spinach pie in filo
spetzofáï sausage and peppers in spicy sauce
stafúlia grapes
ste soúvla spit roast
stifádo meat stew with shallots
sto foúrno baked in the oven
strídia oysters
talagoútes small thick (sweet) pancakes
taramosaláta fish roe paste dip
thalasiná seafood
tiganitá/és/ó (all variations mean 'fried')
tirí cheese
tirokeftédes cheese balls
tirópita cheese pie
tirosaláta spicy cheese dip
tónnos tuna
tost toast
tsáï tea
tzatzíki yoghurt, garlic, cucumber dip

vradinó evening meal
vrastó boiled
yaoúrti yoghurt
yemistá/és/ó (all variations mean 'stuffed')
youvétsi veal stew with *manéstra*
zambon ham
zákari sugar
zesté sokoláta hot chocolate

SHOPPING TERMS

allspice *bakári* (whole or ground)
apples *méla*
apricot *veríkoko*
aubergine *melitzána*
bananas *banánes*
basil *vasilikós*
bay leaf *dáfne*
beans, french *fasolákia*
beans, broad *koukiá*
beef *moskári*
beer *bíra*
bread *psomí*
bread (olive) *elioté*
butter *voútero*
cabbage *lákano*
cake *pásta*
carrots *karóta*
cheese *tirí*
cherries *kerásia*
chestnut *kastaniá*
chicken *kotópoulo*
chickpeas *revíthia*

chocolate *kakáo*
chop *brizóla*
cinnamon *kanéla*
coffee *kafé*
  instant *nes*
courgettes *kolokithákia*
cream *kréma*
cucumber *angoúri*
cutlets *kotolétes*
dips
  aubergine *melitzá- nosaláta*
  fish roe paste *tara- mosaláta*
  garlic/mashed potato *skordaliá*
  spicy cheese *tiro- saláta*
  yoghurt/garlic/ cucumber *tzatzíki*
eggs *avgá*
feta cheese *féta*
filet *filéto*
fish *psári*
  cod, dried *baka- liáros*
  cod, fresh *galéos*
  sword *ksifías*
  tuna *tónnos*
  whitebait-type *marídes*
flour *alévri*
fresh *fréska*
frozen *katepsig- méno*
fruit *froúta*
garlic *skórdo*
grapes *stafélia*
ham *zambón*
honey *méli*

ice
  cubes *pagákia*
  cream *pagotó*
lamb *arní*
lettuce *maroúli*
liver *sikóti*
margarine *margaríni*
meat *kréas*
  on a skewer, for barbecuing *souvláki*
melon (water) *karpoúzi*
melon *pepóni*
milk *gála*
mince *kimás*
mushrooms *manitária*
mussels *múdia*
octopus *oktapódi*
oil *ládi*
  olive *elaiólado*
olives *eliés*
onions *kremédia*
oranges *portokáli*
oregano *rígani*
oysters *strídia*
parsley *maïdanós*
pastry *pastá*
peach *rodákino*
peas *arakás*
pepper *pipéri*
peppers *piperiés*
pork *hoirinó*
potatoes *patátes*
prawns or shrimps *garídes*
rabbit *kounéli*
rice *piláfi*
rosemary *dendro-*

lívano
salad *saláta*
salt *aláti*
sardines *sardélles*
sausage *loukániko*
  home-made *seftaliá*
seafood *thalasiná*
shrimps (small, sweet, from Sími) *simiakó*
snails *saligária*
soup *soúpa*
spaghetti *makarónia*
spinach *spanáki*
squid *kalamária*
sugar *zákari*
strawberries *fráoules*
tea *tsäï*
tomatoes *domátes*
turkey *galopoúla*
veal *moskári*
vinegar *ksúdi* (pronounced *kseethi*)
walnuts *karídes* (pronounced *kareethi*)
water *neró*
wine *krasí*
  white *áspero krasí*
  red *kókkino krasí*
  rosé *rozé krasí*
yoghurt *yiaoúrti*
general
bottle *boukáli*
kilo *kiló*
half-kilo *misó kiló*
carrier bag *sakoúla*

bold type: photograph; *italic type:* map

INDEX

Third edition © 2022
Published by Sunflower Books
PO Box 36061, London SW7 3WS
www.sunflowerbooks.co.uk

ISBN 978-1-85691-543-4

Cover photograph: Mandráki Harbour entrance
Photographs: Brian and Eileen Anderson
Maps for Walks 1, 2 and 12: Sunflower Books, adapted from Road Edition and
    old military maps. Maps for Walks 3-11: Jan Kostura (see pages 28 and 29),
    with contour data by Nick Hill, made available under ODbL (opendatacommons.
    org/licenses/odbl/1.0)
Series design: Jocelyn Lucas
Cookery editor: Marina Bayliss
A CIP catalogue record for this book is available from the British Library.
Printed and bound in England by Short Run Press, Exeter

Before you go ...
log on to
www.sunflowerbooks.co.uk
and click on '**updates**', to see if we have been notified of any changes to
the routes or restaurants.

When you return ...
do let us know if any routes have changed because of road-building, storm
damage or the like. Have any of our restaurants closed — or any new ones
opened *on the route of the walk*? (Not Rhodes Town restaurants, please; these
books are not intended to be complete restaurant guides!)
Send your comments to info@sunflowerbooks.co.uk